T0115395

RESILIENCE AND SUCCESS OF AFRICAN AMERICAN PASTORS

A Phenomenological Investigation

DR. TERENCE O. HAYES, SR.

WESTBOW
PRESS®
A DIVISION OF THOMAS NELSON
& ZONDERVAN

WestBow Press books may be ordered through booksellers or by contacting:

WestBow Press
A Division of Thomas Nelson & Zondervan
1663 Liberty Drive
Bloomington, IN 47403
www.westbowpress.com
844-714-3454

Because of the dynamic nature of the Internet, any web addresses or
links contained in this book may have changed since publication and
may no longer be valid. The views expressed in this work are solely those
of the author and do not necessarily reflect the views of the publisher,
and the publisher hereby disclaims any responsibility for them.

Any people depicted in stock imagery provided by Getty Images are
models, and such images are being used for illustrative purposes only.
Certain stock imagery © Getty Images.

tohayes61@gmail.com

Scripture quotations taken from The Holy Bible, New International
Version® NIV® Copyright © 1973 1978 1984 2011 by Biblica, Inc.
TM. Used by permission. All rights reserved worldwide.

"Scripture quotations taken from the (NASB®) New American Standard
Bible®, Copyright © 1960, 1971, 1977, 1995, 2020 by The Lockman
Foundation. Used by permission. All rights reserved. www.lockman.org"

Scripture taken from the King James Version of the Bible.

ISBN: 978-1-6642-3010-1 (sc)
ISBN: 978-1-6642-3012-5 (hc)
ISBN: 978-1-6642-3011-8 (e)

Library of Congress Control Number: 2021907011

Print information available on the last page.

WestBow Press rev. date: 04/21/2021

DEDICATION

This book is dedicated to the love of my life, Rhonda L. McDuffie-Hayes who has shared the blessings of our lives together of over forty years of holy matrimony. To all of my adult children, Sharita, Terence, Shawnda, Alisha (Jarre) Latosha, Troy (Dani) and Tanesha (Brandon); all of you are greatly loved. To all the Hayes' grandchildren; Nana and Papa love you dearly. Lastly, to the Faith Deliverance Church of God in Christ family, I am humbled to serve you.

In loving memory of my loving mother, Ethel Hayes; my heartbeat, my father; my music inspiration.

The Biblical verse that saved my life:

"Thou wilt keep him in perfect peace, whose mind is stayed on thee: because he trusteth in thee. (Isaiah 26:3, KJV)

CONTENTS

TABLES

ABSTRACT

The content of this manuscript is research investigated for the resilience and success of pastors in the Church of God in Christ, a Pentecostal denomination that has more than six million members, to include more than three thousand pastors. The research is a phenomenological study designed to provide a narrative interview of the participants to share their background, role, and day-to-day practices of the work of ministry as a senior pastor in this organization. The research will consist of seven to ten pastors selected from across the country, all African American males, age groups ranging from forty-two years to seventy-two years of age. The information will be gathered by personal interviews conducted, asking each of them the same questions to gather all the facts and data for this research design. The instrument used will be a recording device that will record all conversations, which will then be transcribed in writing verbatim. As the human instrument conducting this research, it will constitute travel, lodging, and scheduling of each participant that will give the researcher intimate and close contact with each participant. The information will be safeguarded, names will be protected, and all information will be useful as a model example of what constitutes success for ministry and the tools and resources needed to maintain a healthy and productive state of mind to be resilient in leading the charge as clergymen in the field of ministry. It is with great joy and a privilege to conduct this interview with pastors serving in the Church of God in Christ.

Keywords: Success, Resilience, Pastors, Investigation, Pentecostal, Denomination

1

INTRODUCTION

Overview

The calling of God on the life of a man or woman in the work of ministry is a tasking that only the hand of God can make known into the lives of those called to serve and commit to this work. "Serving as a pastor (or church leader) in a local church is a special and wonderful calling from God to shepherd his people or flock" (Tan 2019, 3). It is more than a job; it's a vocation designed for those who have a love for God and a strong love for people. The calling of God in a pastor's life is comparable to a summons. Barth asserts, "Each person has a distinct vocation that is the basis for obedience to the divine summons" (Joynt 2019, 113). It is not for the faint of heart, for the journey can be a monumental walk with a heartfelt, heart-warming determination that leads to something with an assurance that this role is the one for the right person. The ultimate goal for pastors is to make this work with a stake of professionalism while simultaneously serving to be effective and bring forth a state of excellence in this position (Muhammad 2018).

Further research on the topic of establishing the success and role of pastors in one of the largest Pentecostal movements in Christendom is by way of the Church of God in Christ. Many of the clergymen in this group are ordained and appointed to serve as

1

pastors—ministers without any formal theological education. To deny a person their calling in this denomination would be a travesty before God because a call to them comes directly from God. The research revealed how men and women defend their identities in this field despite the educational deficiencies, restricted labor market, and gender discrimination, which threatens the legitimacy and their desire to walk into their calling as clergymen (Pitt 2012). Pitt writes, "Most Protestant denominations affirm the idea that there must be a specific encounter with God that leads people to devote their lives to ministry" (Pitt 2012, 9). This "call to ministry" brings legitimacy to the Lord's work they are committed to doing in their everyday lives (Pitt 2012).

Success does not happen without any effort, any direct focus, or from longing and passion that cannot be quenched just by imagining. It has to be active, driven, and purposeful. The clergymen in the Church of God in Christ see the passion in a different light. In the body of Christ, there is what is known as the laity—the men and women who are members of a local congregation. When a person has a passion to move beyond the pews of just attending, their passion kicks into another drive. The men in ministry see their lives as set apart from their peers, and they are called to a higher level of passion for the work of ministry than those who are unlicensed in the church (Pitt 2012). Further, the passion is a heightened view for their commitment and dedication to the work of ministry, which gives their excitement and joy of ministry the sustenance and endurance it needs to stay the course (Pitt 2012).

"Every successful journey requires a starting point, an ending point, and a reason" (Moore 2017, 3). The journey to explore the engagement and successes of one of the leading Pentecostal movements in the world will provide valuable research and a map for pastors hoping to be on the cutting edge and stand head-to-head with great men around the globe.

There needs to be a clear distinction between being successful and being professional as it pertains to ministry. One of the most respected authors of pastoral care is John Piper. His spiritual view of professionalism is greatly noted from a spiritual and godly perspective. "We pastors are being killed by the professionalizing of the pastoral ministry … Professionalism has nothing to do with the essence and heart of the Christian ministry" (Tan 2019, 12). Being knowledgeable and skillful, and having our competence and abilities doesn't make us experts in ministry (Tan 2019). In many Christian denominations, they have to convince a credentialing body that they have received a vertical call (Pitt 2012, 43). To some, this type of call is downplayed if it does not include some explicitly supernatural experience (Pitt 2012).

Ordination is an important sanctioning of men called into ministry. Once a minister carries out the training and principles required of them to become licensed, the next step is to pursue the official stamp of approval of their divine calling. "Clergy in denominations like COGIC are more likely than the others to cite the importance of their conviction that God wishes them to be ordained and their belief that through the ordained ministry they can serve God better" (Pitt 2012, 45).

Background

The ministerial credentials are important and relevant for the men who are called of God to serve in ministry in the Church of God in Christ. The first credential is that of receiving a license as a minister. The pastor of the congregation labels him as an "aspiring minister" until he proves and affirms he has been called of God. "To qualify for a ministerial license, he should be personally convinced of his call to ministry … be able to convince others that God called him to preach, possess a holy conversation, a sound understanding of the things of God, and have a good report of those within and without" (Pitt 2012, 31). The minister must further exhibit his steadfastness, resilience, and dedication to studying, to show himself approved in the word of God. After one year, he is then granted an official license to preach but only to the lay members. He is further allowed to preach in his local church, prisons, and hospitals, as a representative of his church (Pitts 2012). There are other duties assigned that he can conduct in the name of the ministry until he is awarded the title of an ordained elder. Pastors are in one of the most rewarding roles of ministry one can undertake.

It is the pastor who has the responsibility to feed, lead, and serve the flock of God with dedication, commitment, and focus unlike any other work in a ministry. The desire to see a congregation grow, mature, and display the life of Christ in their everyday behavior is a sign of ultimate success as the voice and leader needed in the work of a church. This work requires someone with the resilience and fortitude to begin a work with the vision to complete the task well. After serving willingly and untiringly as a pastor who gives the best of their strength, labor, and heart, there comes the time to hand the baton over to the next leader to take the ministry to another level. To be successful and to earn the honor of becoming a successful senior pastor, in the end, is the ultimate focus of this research. This achievement does not happen overnight. To achieve greatness takes time, diligent study, and a prolonged period to develop (Muhammad 2018).

Ministry requires a true commitment and dedication to the work of service. The words of Timothy read, "Let the elders that rule well be counted worthy of double honor, especially they who labor in the word and doctrine" (1 Timothy 5:17 KJV). A senior pastor has labored untiringly. He or she has given of themselves, their families, and their lives for the call they surrendered to for God. Some studies reveal there are positive benefits to the pastoral role. Of this group of protestant pastors, they argued that ministry is a "deeply satisfying calling" (Lee 2010).

Problem Statement

Research in the work of the ministry has shown "clergy are leaving the ministry in greater numbers than ever before as a significant and increasing cross-section of evangelical clergy express a growing sense of spiritual, physical, emotional, and social bombardment (Spencer, Winston, and Bocarnea 2011, 85). A study conducted at Duke University unveiled that 85 percent of seminary graduates who enter into ministry will depart within five years. And 90 percent of most pastors will not stay until retirement (Stewart 2009). It is very concerning and thus necessary to seek the reason such a high number of men and women are walking away from this tasking after investing the time, study, and preparation for their ministry. However, some start in ministry, and the path they take is filled with joy, happiness, and fulfillment. They have found a way to navigate the terrain of ministry and make it a successful profession or career.

The discussion of the various reasons ministry encounters challenges and the necessity for ministers to monitor their spiritual, relational, psychological, and physical well-being is important to reach the level of a good run during the tenure in ministry (Reed 2016). Maintaining the right structure and implementing the right procedures and behaviors, along with the tools that are available to assist pastors or clergymen to hold on to the reins of ministry, are crucial. It is important to build a strong network of solid relationships to protect clergy from emotional and physical exhaustion that leads to burnout (Jackson-Jordan 2013). It is with this study that the commitment to produce the research can be a model for persons to succeed in the role of ministry. Some pastors appear to have the ability to overcome obstacles and challenges and to continue on to fruitful and long-term ministry. The research seeks to discover and encompass the words of Jesus when he says the gates of hell will not prevail against the church we inherited from the apostles. Now that's resilience (Barna 2017, 160).

Purpose Statement

The purpose of this study is to determine what is required for pastors to become successful in ministry, to endure the road of ministry with a long-term tenure and gain the respect and reward bestowed upon them to become a tenured senior pastor in the Church of God in Christ Pentecostal Denomination. Becoming a senior pastor comes through a mindset of knowing the role and place one has been called to be effective. "Effective means choosing the right thing to do for ourselves" (Luciotti 2019, 12). The question that will be defined in this research is "What determines success? Pastors lead churches; a church is successful having the power of the Spirit of God assisting the ministry to accomplish their mission without lowering the ministry values" (Malphurs 2013, 149). The persons who sit at the head of the table must be disciplined, focused, and committed and have the assurance the work they are doing in ministry is a work that they must do as servants and stewards of the kingdom of God. The research will further examine how some pastors work through difficulty and earn the title to become a senior pastor. Just as athletes earn gold medals, a pastor who has served faithfully and diligently in ministry during their lifetime should merit the honor of being called senior pastor. The work of a pastor is not easy. "True shepherds are willing to bear the scars, the disappointments, and the hardships of the task because they care deeply for their sheep" (Tan 2019, 11).

The growth of a ministry is not the role of the pastor. The church belongs to God. The fruit of a pastor's labor is indicative of his or her ultimate success. "God is not unjust; he will not forget your work and love you have shown Him as you have helped his people and continue to help them" (Hebrews 6:10 NIV). According to Burns, Chapman, and Gutherie (2013), there was some evidence of numerical success, and faithfulness was helpful, but neither of these two measures was efficient enough to assess the idea of excellence.

The best way to see a clearer picture of success is by fruitfulness (Burns et al.).

Significance of the Study

The desire to see men and women succeed in the work of ministry in total excellence and great significance is important for those who are considering to walk into this role after years of study in seminary, having a personal ambition to fulfill a call on their life and have the assurance with Christ they can do all things possible with him dwelling on the inside of their hearts. "The key to successful spiritual leadership has much more to do with the leader's internal life than with the leaders' expertise, gifts, or experience" (Scazzero 2010, 20). The impact of this study can have a positive outcome as a means to examine the heart and passion of what ministry should be. A shepherd's heart moves the heart and mind of God. The Word of God is the compass that provides the order and perspective of what it looks like to serve as a pastor, which comes from the biblical perspective of the scriptures (Tan 2019).

Historically, pastors have been among the most influential leaders in the nation (Barna 2017, 106). A further study of this research will influence current and future generations of pastors with significant and valuable information so they, too, can become long-term, successful pastors.

Research Questions

The questions for this research are birthed from the desire to know the success and mindset of a driven and focused leader who navigates through the deep waters of ministry. "Many emerging or reemerging leaders do whatever it takes within their organization to reach a position of influence and to stay there. They call this success" (Thrall, McNicol, and McElrath 1999, 22). Success also breeds effectiveness. "Across all functions and church sizes, skills of intentional leadership were found to be most predictive of pastoral effectiveness" (McKenna and Eckard 2009, 304). A pastor's effectiveness encompasses preaching and the relationship he has with a congregation. Therefore, effectiveness has been analyzed as an individual construct (McKenna and Eckard 2009). It is with these questions the researcher is seeking to know what makes a leader last:

1. What is it about ministry that gave some pastors the resilience and tenacity to become a long-tenured pastor?
2. What gave some pastors the strength and ability to work through difficulty that earned them the title of senior pastor?
3. What are the innate talents or abilities possessed by some pastors and implemented in their ministry that enabled a long-term tenure?

Locating Self as a Researcher

The focus of this research addresses the role, leadership, and function of male pastors. In this twenty-first century, the world has progressed, and women are taking a strong presence in leadership roles. The Church of God in Christ has both men and women in ministry. However, men are the only ones who are ordained and appointed as senior pastors. It is worth observing, "What is clear is that women's roles in the Church of God in Christ have emerged over the decades … and they continue to evolve" (Johnson, Hall, Daniels, and Herndon 2019, 302). The role of women in ministry further reveals "but nowhere can we find a mandate to ordain women to be an Elder, Bishop or Pastor" (Johnson, Hall, Daniels, and Herndon 2019, 303). The nation just elected its first female vice president, Senator Kamala Harris. It is interesting to observe where women in the Church of God in Christ may view this moment of history for consideration of women to be ordained in this African American Pentecostal movement. Qualitative inquiry is an interactive and transformational process in which the researcher seeks to learn about and interpret life experiences (Sword 2019, 270). Women are able to assist in the work of ministry and help pastors do the work effectively, without a charge. In qualitative study, the researcher's curiosity, relationships with participants, and conceptual lenses through which data are gathered and interpreted have significant bearing on the research (Sword 2019, 270). Further research is merited to explore this gender gap.

Definitions

The following terms are pertinent to this study and are listed to define the meaning of the terms that will be used throughout the study.

1. Pastoral excellence: "Christian leaders are to bear fruit by sharing their faith and nurturing the fruit of God's grace in their own lives and the lives of others. Fruitfulness includes a measure of faithfulness and a measure of success-valuing both but preferring neither" (Burns, Chapman, and Gutherie 2013, 13).
2. Spiritual formation: "The ongoing process of maturing as a Christian, both personally and interpersonally. The key to this definition is the phrase process of maturing" (Burns, Chapman, and Gutherie 2013, 19).
3. Self-care: "The ideas of self-care involve the pursuit of physical, mental and emotional health" (Burns, Chapman, and Gutherie 2013, 21).
4. Emotional intelligence: "The ability to proactively respond to one's own emotions" (Burns, Chapman, and Gutherie 2013, 24).

5. Cultural intelligence: "It is the ability to recognize and adapt to different cultural contexts" (Burns, Chapman, and Gutherie 2013, 24).

6. Pastor: "The word 'pastor' transliterated from the Latin word *pastor,* actually means 'shepherd,' with the connotation of feeding a flock of sheep" (Tan 2019, 9).

7. Leadership: "Leadership is a dynamic process in which a man or woman with God-given capacity influences a specific group to God's people toward His purposes for the group" (Tan 2019, 115).

8. Tenure: A period for which an office is held (dictionary.com).

Summary

The tenure of pastors is a reality that is taking place in ministries across the country. Men and women have dedicated their lives to a work of ministry with the passion, tenacity, and faith in God to reach a major milestone of doing the Lord's business. Through the tests and trials of ministry, the road signs are visible from the many factual and powerful narratives written in the chronicles of the Bible, which were written for the learning and witness to the work of ministry that has been known to humankind. The wise words of Solomon read: "If thou faint in the day of adversity, thy strength is small" (Proverbs 24:10 KJV). It takes focus and a determined will to succeed in ministry. "If a leader shows strong discipline, others will see it and cooperate with the expectations placed on them" (Sanders 2007, 64).

From the research to date, the gap and research merit more work to be accomplished. The research question is the focus and guides an investigation that must be carefully constructed, every word deliberately chosen and ordered in such a way that the primary words appear immediately, capture the attention, and guide one in the phenomenological process of seeing, reflecting, and knowing (Moustakas 1994, 59).

2

LITERATURE REVIEW

Overview

The literature for this review addresses the successes and challenges many pastors encounter when serving in the role of pastor, clergy, chaplain, or priest for a long-term role. Decline in ministry is a sign that there is a need for research to address a problem that has affected the work of ministry. Research conducted by the Barna Group has shown the majority of Protestant churches in America have been in a pattern of decline (Strunk, Milacci, and Zabloski 2017). Two crises came to the forefront of reduction in ministry in the world; the first was the social demographic changes from the baby boomers, and the second was the identity within the churches as well as how the mainline churches were able to adapt and adjust to the cultural changes (Strunk, Milacci, and Zabloski 2017).

Further exploration of this crisis raises the interest as to what makes a ministry successful and resilient and what qualifications and means bring this into fruition. Research states, "Extensive studies conducted over the last decade and a half have indicated that deficiency in pastoral leadership is also often a key contributor to a lack of congregational vitality" (Strunk, Milacci, and Zabloski 2017, 538). Vitality is defined as the state of being strong and active; energy (Dictionary). The years given to ministry show the resilience and vitality the pastor has in the role of his or her work. Malphrus states it takes five to ten years to move from just being the preacher to evolving into the pastor, as the title of a pastor is not the same as the role (Strunk, Milacci, and Zabloski 2017). There are many reasons and factors that define church vitality. A long journey for pastoral tenure of five or more years of service on the surface appears to be an important ingredient of church vitality (Strunk, Milacci, and Zabloski 2017). The ability to weather the cycle of serving as a pastor in a successful and long-lasting tenure requires further study.

Conceptual or Theoretical Framework

Gerald Corey writes that theoretical integration refers to a conceptual or theoretical creation beyond a mere blending of techniques (Corey 2009, 449). This theoretical concept further states, "This route has the goal of producing a conceptual framework that synthesis the best aspects of two or more theoretical approaches under the assumption that the outcome will be richer than either theory alone" (Corey 2009, 449). The personality and resolve that mark the identity of pastors in ministry are centered on the theoretical view of Alfred Adler. The Alderian theory offers some insight into this framework with individual psychology.

Individual psychology sheds the light on an optimistic view of people, leaning on the thoughts of social interest, which provides a feeling of oneness for humankind (Feist, Feist, and Roberts 2013). Resilient pastors must have an optimistic view of the things they encounter in life. Alder saw people inspired and motivated by their social engagement and how they strived to be successful. He said people are accountable and responsible for who they are, and present behavior defines people's view of their future. And lastly, Adler believed that, psychologically, people who are healthy are very aware of what they are doing and the purpose of why they are doing it (Feist, Feist, and Roberts 2013).

Adler's close call with death in his childhood was the motivation that gave him the desire to become a physician. It is through trial, hardships, and setbacks that a resilient attitude comes to the surface. The biblical principle reads, "If thou faint in the day of adversity, thy strength is small" (Proverbs 24:10 KJV). From his brush with death, he believed people are born with weak, inferior bodies, which leads to the feeling of inferiority and the need to depend on other people (Feist, Feist, and Roberts 2013). His belief in unity is the same view pastors desire to see among the men and women in a congregation. It is further noted he was not rooted in a religious background; however, he did become acquainted with Protestantism. In his literary works, the Bible was part of how he shared life experiences.

There are five tenets of the Adlerian theory: 1) the one dynamic force behind people's behavior is the *striving for success or superiority*; 2) people's *subjective perceptions* shape their behavior and personality; 3) personality is *unified and self-consistent*; 4) the value of all human activity must be seen from the viewpoint of *social interests*; 5) the self-consistent personality structure develops into a person's *style of life*; 6) style of life is molded by people's *creative power* (Feist, Feist, and Roberts 2013, 73–74).

The work of Bandura addresses the theoretical framework of the social cognitive theory. One thing is certain: pastors have lived experiences with the congregation, and you never know what will happen in real time, but the ability to adapt, adjust, and press through is clear in these circumstances. There are several assumptions, according to Bandura, that take place with this theory: plasticity, triadic reciprocal causation, agentic perspective, external factors, and moral agency. One key view from this framework self-efficacy (Feist, Feist, and Roberts 2013).

Self-Efficacy

"Bandura defined self-efficacy as 'people's beliefs in their capability to exercise some measure of control over their own functioning and over environmental events'" (Feist, Feist, and Roberts, 2013, 493). He further states, which drives a key element of when resiliency at its finest moment will rise, "People's beliefs in their personal efficacy influence what courses of action they choose to pursue, how much effort they will invest in activities, how long they will persevere in the face of obstacles and failure experiences, and their resiliency follow setbacks" (Feist, Feist, and Roberts 2013, 493). The lived experiences from pastors will make the research that much more meaningful, informative, relatable, and relevant for the study. "Any lived-experience description is an appropriate source for uncovering thematic aspects of the phenomenon it describes. But is true that some descriptions are richer than others" (Manen 2015, 92).

There are gaps in the research to reveal all of the successful areas of leadership and resilience that are modeled in the lives of pastors today. Longevity is paramount to map out the destiny of successful pastors. The African American pastors in the Church of God in Christ are the focus of this research to determine the mechanism, fortitude, and passion needed for persons serving in ministry to have a successful and resilient attitude while leading the men, women, families, and children pastors have been called to serve. The call, the voice, the desire that these men and women heard and adhered to justified their role, relationship, and ability to lead as the representatives and servants of the Lord. Success has to be determined by what it looks like and how easy or difficult it might be to achieve. Having a humble understanding of being a pastor is important to have the right view of the calling of ministers (Wilson and Hoffman 2007). Adler further states, "Success is an individualized concept and all people formulate their own definition of it" (Feist, Feist, and Roberts 2013, 76).

The investigative approach for this research is to address how resilience and grit are the driving means to keep pastors grounded, focused, and committed to serving even through trying, difficult, and exciting times. It is about surviving and thriving at the same time.

There are five themes centered on the elements that comprise the components of a resilient ministry: a) spiritual formation, b) self-care, c) emotional and cultural intelligence, d) marriage and family, e) leadership and management (Burns, Chapman, and Guthrie 2013).

Barna conducted research on the state of pastors, which covered traits of a resilient leader, as shown in table 1, answering the question: "One who ..."

Table 1. Five traits of resilience

a) prioritizes their own spiritual emotional and physical needs	b) views challenges realistically	c) learns from their mistakes	d) considers alternate perspectives and new processes	e) expects that God is at work even in adverse situations

(Barna 2017, 156)

It is with great expectations the results of this research will become a model and inspiration for pastors serving in the Church of God in Christ to become successful and resilient in their profession.

Literature Review

Resilient and Thriving in Ministry

Thriving leadership is contagious. Every leader wants to feel in charge and in control of making things happen in the place of ministry he is serving. It has been said, "When pastors are thriving, they are energized and joyful. It is out of this kind of energy a congregation responds to the leadership they are under" (Steiner 2009). Ministry that is meaningful and purposeful gives life and a strong constitution to bring good things to life. A key element to keep a pastor on the cutting edge of excellence is a continued mind to grow in Christ, putting prayer at the top of the list to maintain a strong, healthy spiritual life (Steiner 2017). A prayer life with reading the Word of God keeps men in ministry grounded and focused. It is needful to implement any spiritual disciplines, including fasting, devotions, worship, exercise, and the like. Another key discipline for a successful pastor is having trustworthy mentors and coaches in an inner circle (Steiner 2017). Jesus had twelve disciples, but he had an inner circle with three specific disciples, Peter, James, and John. It is important to take time to refresh and reenergize the mind in ministry. The fact that Jesus had twelve disciples adds substance to the fact pastors need one another. Perseverance goes a long way in supporting one another in ministry, as it is not a one-man function but a corporate one (Emlet 2017). Ministry requires giving of one's self; therefore, one must lead healthily and productively, develop a rhythm of life, and protect it well (Steiner 2017).

Resilience

Resilience is defined by Dekker as "the ability to thrive, mature and increase competence in the face of adverse circumstances or obstacles" (Dekker 2011, 68). Resilience is defined as "the process of overcoming the negative effects of risk exposure, coping successfully with traumatic experiences, and avoiding the negative trajectories associated with risk" (Dekker 2011, 68). *The Resilience Handbook* addresses three elements of importance: resilience with sustainability that moves forward despite the challenge; a bounce-back mentality and recovery from any challenge; and in the process of learning and growth, new knowledge and new skills (Schuhmann and Geugten 2017). Ministry encompasses the unexpected, unknown, and challenges that cannot keep it moving successfully. In the mix of pastoral care for students studying social work, it is highly encouraged to promote resilience as a protective trait, with the understanding that resilience is the personal capacity to change and manage internal and external stressors (Schuhmann and Geugten 2017). There must be supporting social environments when it comes to the guidance and development of pastoral care (Schuhmann and Geugten 2017).

From a Christian theological perspective, the term resilience is defined as "the motivational force within everyone that drives them to pursue wisdom, self-actualization, and altruism and to be in harmony with a spiritual source of strength" (Dillen 2012, 61)

Preparation for Ministry

Preparation is required to step into the office of a pastor on day one. It is a job that requires one to serve with a twenty-four seven attitude, having in place a good infrastructure with solid boundaries to keep balance and good self-care in the fold. Pastors must be wise and have the conviction that wise leadership begins early in their call and creates an atmosphere of great leadership through daily habits that are fruitful for ministry (Scharen and Campbell-Reed 2017). Many pastors share their preparation, for the work of the ministry is more about information than formation (Scharen and Campbell-Reed 2017). The objective is to put it into place by any means deemed appropriate, to see the growth and movement of ministry. Amid resilience and determination of ministers, pastors are finding ways to see the possibility versus ministry falling into despair over brick walls of issues that seek to block them by emerging to the next level using their pastoral imagination (Scharen and Campbell-Reed 2017).

Dr. Terence O. Hayes, Sr.

The Call of Ministry

The call of ministry merits a lot of attention in the work of ministry, identifying a Christian view of vocation, what it is to seek and follow God in the everyday engagement and setting in which life and work take place for ministry (Price 2013).

A qualitative study was conducted of thirty pastors who participated in a conversation and dialogue in the African American community to assess the power of influence displayed by pastors in their perspective communities. The influence of these pastors helped make a difference in the educational needs and better health care for the members of the perspective congregations (Harmon, Strayhorn, Webb, and Hebert 2018).

A research initiative was conducted with eleven women who were interviewed about their longevity in ministry. A follow-up was conducted to learn that, of the eleven women in ministry, one of them retired, and the other women served in other roles outside of ministry. The overall research traces a pastor's call for ministry and how it translates into secular work after leaving a ministry (Bumgardner 2016).

The tasking to determine how effective and successful the work of a musical pastor is in ministry is the purview of this research. Three specific areas that are covered are personal/spiritual maturity, ministerial identity, and praxis. The foundation for a well-rounded ministry is to maintain balance and focused engagement (Barton 2017).

An authentic leadership questionnaire was used to measure the authentic leadership and the relationship pastors have with the lay members, to clearly define the effectiveness of their ministries. Four areas measured for the questionnaire were: self-awareness, internalized moral perspective, balanced processing, and relational transparency (Pulls, Ludden, and Freemyer 2014)

The stories involving the research of ten pastors serving their congregations for the past twenty years reveals the practices that proved successful, influential, and relevant for the congregants they have served. Developing a close relationship with God, connections with family, and self care are all part of establishing a well-rooted ministry (Reed 2016).

Pastors in Ministry

It takes self-discipline and drive to lead and serve people in ministry today. Most pastors who have resiliency running in their veins are settled, are strong in their home life, have a great excitement in their pursuit of God, conduct their finances well, keep their mental and emotional equilibrium in check, are willing to learn new things, and have a confidence in their ministry calling (Barna 2017). In today's society, many pastors consider what it means to practice self-leadership. "The 'self' in 'self-leadership' should not imply that spiritual leaders are or should be on their own—far from it" (Barna 2017, 156).

Many clergies heed to the call of ministry because they feel they have been called to serve churches, and they rely on God to cover their inadequacy or insufficiency. They journey onward to make a great impact in their ministry, but it is a known fact they experience burnout (Barnard and Curry 2011).

Research has been conducted to determine why pastors walk away from ministry. The study reveals the various reasons one chooses to step away. Most who walk away do not return to any form of ministry into the church. The most common reason is the lack of preparation (Stewart 2009). This is just one of many reasons to be revealed and discovered.

In research on burnout, the Maslach Burnout Inventory (MBI) is a well-known instrument used in the field of caring professions (Randall 2013). Clergymen have a shepherd's heart; this is where the care aspect is adapted for this vocation. Three crucial elements were identified to measure burnout with this instrument: emotional exhaustion, development of depersonalization, and a reduced sense of personal accomplishment (Kendall 2013).

The pilot study of twenty-four pastors examined the factors that affect the resilience and fortitude of these men serving in ministry. Three important elements reviewed were social environment, dispositional resiliency, and pastoral adjustment. A random nonsampling of these men measured good data for this study (Lee 2010).

The importance of assessing accurate and concise information is predicated on having important data to definitively provide a clear and true hypothesis testing results. Seven respondents failed to give the current data needed to help in assessing the self-disclosure of the well-being of a pastor's psychological mental health (Salween, Underwood, Dy-Liacco, and Arveson 2017).

This research reveals the crisis of a pastor leading an Australian Lutheran church. In his search for leading, there has been a decline in ministry, and he has taken some personal time to access his personal life. The ultimate questions are centered on how one guards against depression in ministry, should a doubling down be made for expectations, and how the Gospel transforms a community (Braunack-Mayer 2018).

Relational connection with pastors reveals three areas in a qualitative relational study: pastors need to have intentional relationships, pastors need to be available to their congregation, and pastors need to give attention to connecting with lay church leaders (Young and Firmin 2014). The role of leadership is important in the calling of ministry. When reviewing the pastoral leadership effectiveness, their spiritual state must be examined as well (Carter 2009). Pastors must ensure they are meditating in the Word of God for the successful work of ministry (McGrath-Merkle 2011).

Service in Ministry

It has been declared there are not many interventions to show how positive an impact it is in ministry for pastors to remain in this professional field as a clergyman (Stewart 2009). It is from the love, passion, and call of God these men and women are leading the charge to serve the people they have been called to minister to. If former pastors overwhelmingly affirm they had a call from God to serve, perhaps these men can be a voice to encourage men and women who leave to stay for the long haul (Stewart 2009). In the secular world, a person takes a job with all the hope and aspirations to stay and retire from the company. The benefits alone create enough chemistry to make that job become a dream job. A study conducted by Duke University argued, "Ministry is a deeply satisfying calling for a majority of those who participated in the research. 70% had never considered leaving pastoral ministry" (Lee 2010, 631). Pastors who flourish in ministry come with one exclusive and unique flair: despite some difficulties in the pastoral role, a faithful sense of call to shepherd the people of God with joy and passion (Adams and Bloom 2017). The good work of a great pastor brings forth the real goodness of many kinds (Adams and Bloom 2017). Well-being is a notable attribute to have in ministry. Along with happiness, flourishing, and a positive professional image, there is another key characteristic to describe a strong leader: resilience. "By resilience, we mean a person's capacity to respond to the changing and sometimes challenging world around them" (Adams and Bloom 2017, 256). Three terms extend the meaning of resilience: self-awareness, self-reflectivity, and self-control (Adams and Bloom 2017). To define what is deemed successful for ministry is a matter of interpretation. Notwithstanding, every pastor has not been successful in serving in ministry. Research reveals the calling for one to follow God as a believer is not only empowering but very purposeful. The call of God is necessary to accomplish the work without fail, and the task to do the work is a divine call of God needed in the world (Price 2013).

For Calvin, "the candidate could be assured that he is truly called by God, not based on a strong, inward call, but on the outward call of the church based upon an objective assessment of their suitability" (Tucker 2017, 103).

The pastor who serves a community and operates with those he served in a faith community functions as following God's call (Manala 2010). To live on purpose gives one the determination, fortitude, and magnitude to do whatever is essential and important to have an impact in the lives of the people a leader is called to serve. Knowing the call and identifying the drive and tenacity it takes to move forward can only be a God-given assignment. Pastors are known for their powerful and charismatic exegesis and preaching and teaching of the Word of God. "It is necessary that the good which is displayed in the life of the pastor should also be propagated by his speech" (Puls, Ludden, and Freemyer 2014, 58).

Mentoring in Ministry

Mentoring is another aspect of serving and being successful in ministry. There is a generation that needs to have a pattern of good works, a model to emulate, and the fortitude to make the difference in those coming behind them. Pastors are not solely obligated to mentor youth; however, they should be available if needed (Price 2013). The Bible describes the young man who was riding on the chariot and did not have anyone to interpret the Word of God he was reading. In his innocence, he spoke up and made it clear. "How can I," he said, "unless someone explains it to me?" (Acts 8:31 NIV). It is in this same framework of thinking that mentoring works to a generation stepping into the role of a successful and engaging leader. Leaders lead. Shepherds of Christ's flock are to lead his flock (Elkington, Meekins, Breen, and Martin 2015, 3). The successful outcome of leaders taking the oversight or charge of the flock they lead comes with the knowledge and ability to do what they are designed to do. "True leadership requires development" (Elkington et.al). The development comes about from many different aspects—higher education, training, conferences, theological training, and leadership training.

Spiritual Maturity

Spiritual maturity is important for the transformation and growth of leaders to stand up to challenges that confront ministry. There must be a resolve so that they will not give up at the drop of uncomfortable circumstances. The best place to find spiritual strength is in the scriptures. The scriptures have encouragement and teaching; they are a guide for how one must conduct their life and a true reality to affirm the life of ministry (Barton 2017). In addressing spiritual maturity, one must acknowledge spiritual formation. There is a lifestyle one must possess; a Christian leader must model the leadership style of a servant like Christ (Adiprasetya 2018). In addition to spiritual maturity, pastors must have space for the full range of self-disclosure, for the simple fact they are expected to set a good example for a congregation to follow (Salwen, Underwood, Dy-Liacco, and Arvenson 2017). Pastors are always on. Even in difficult times, they must be able to have the means to provide the strength they need. Religiosity gives excellent support, which contributes exceptionally well for their well-being (Ngamaba 2014).

Emotional Intelligence

Emotional intelligence covers a wide spectrum of leadership for pastors. "Pastoral ministry is all about relationships. You may be a brilliant theologian, excellent at biblical exegesis, an outstanding preacher, a great pastoral care provider ... but if you are not emotionally intelligent, your ministry as a parish pastor will be difficult" (West 2016, 228). Authentic leaders possess higher emotional intelligence

(Puls, Ludden, and Freemyer 2014). These leaders are self-motivated, love a challenge, are eager to learn, take pride in doing a great job, and have the motivation to do things better (Puls, Ludden, and Freemyer 2014). From all appearances, this is what resilience in leadership looks like too. Resilient and successful pastors must be cognitively sharp, emotionally able, socially engaged, and able to lead people (Puls, Ludden, and Freemyer 2014).

A resilience construct theory provided insight into a recent trend in stress issues that was productive in addressing the problem (Lee 2010). Resilience surrounds both elasticities: having the ability to face a person's level of functioning amid challenges; and buoyancy, having the means to recover or "make a comeback, bounce back" even after encountering disruptions to functioning (Lee 2010). A longitudinal study of children who developed well and thrived in their environment was conducted to show how these children overcame obstacles in their lives (Lee 2010). It goes without saying that the greater amount of supportive relationships pastors have in their congregations, the fewer levels of burnout, which gives a greater outlook for them to remain in ministry (Lee 2010).

There is a distinct difference between resilience and resiliency. "The former refers to actual adaptive processes, while the latter refers to assumed traits or capacities" (Lee 2010, 632). It takes resilience to withstand all that comes along with the work of ministry. Ministry is demanding. It can be tough, but knowing this and how to navigate this gives one the resiliency to win and succeed.

Pastoral Effectiveness

A lot of responsibility lies on the shoulders of pastors today: spiritual guidance and development, motivation, restoration, care, correction, protection, unity, and encouraging the congregation (Carter 2009). The thing at hand for further study is a pastor's effectiveness in the work of ministry beyond the normal day-to-day responsibilities he performs. The effectiveness of a leader is based on the choice of leadership style he chooses to emulate. Two leadership styles revealed in a study are the leadership styles of Moses and Gideon. Leaders with a Moses leadership style are effective at leading previously established groups (Carter 2009). Their character traits include quiet, stable, decisive, sociable, and communicational (Carter 2009). This type of leader is capable of taking over an existing congregation already in place. The Gideon-style leaders are effective and successful in building or establishing a new congregation (Carter 2009). With leadership comes the pressure and need to make the right decision; this is the Gideon leader for sure (Carter 2009). There are more skills necessary to be an effective leader, which brings this research to addressing transformational or transactional leadership. A leader needs to have great social support. The many hours and labor put into the work of ministry require the right amount of structure and balance. The research reveals those in human service occupations have noted social support is instrumental and effective for the successful management of the emotional labor required (Kinman, McFall, and Rodriguez 2011).

One cannot overlook the importance of the personal functioning of pastors. The dynamics of psychology and theology add a great contribution to research by examining the well-being of those who are serving in ministry as the primary spiritual leaders of the church (Hall 1997). There are two reasons for having a balanced and reasonable approach to ministry: the increasing high demand of the pastorate and the impact of personal dysfunction on their ministries (Hall 1997). If one desires to be successful, it is very much doable and possible, but it takes having an awareness that ensures all areas of the ministry are covered. It must be clear that the relative health or dysfunction of the pastor's psychological and spiritual lives can indeed have an impact on the professional effectiveness of serving in ministry (Hall 1997). It is noteworthy to observe coping strategies are important for pastors in ministry. Coping skills are vital for ensuring the resiliency of clergy (Staley, McMinn, Gathercoal, and Free 2012).

Visionary Leaders

Vision is vital to the success and operations of a ministry. "For the vision is yet for an appointed time, but at the end, it shall speak, and not lie: though it tarry, wait for it, because it will surely come, it will not tarry" (Habakkuk 2:3 KJV). Transformational leaders assertively articulate and share a vision that involves the future with their peers and followers (Carter 2009). This type of vision sharing sees the larger picture down the road, not just the present. The transactional leader works and functions within an existing model of operation by maintaining what's working instead of trying to change it (Carter 2009). These styles of leadership are associated with the effectiveness of a leader. The work of the ministry requires men with charisma, fortitude, personality, and the grit to make the work of the ministry sustainable and obtainable for those who are called.

Self-Care in Ministry

One of the best forms of maintaining a healthy and invigorating experience as a pastor is making time for self-care. It has been expressed the primary form of care for all clergymen involves partaking in self-care as well as intrapersonal coping (McMinn, Lish, Trice, Root, Gilbert, and Yap 2005, 576). Hobbies, exercise, and time away from work provide outlets to cope with the day-to-day affairs of ministry (McMinn et al. 2005). Another means of self-care is having good spiritual resources. The time spent in prayer, study, and meditating on the scriptures provides a refreshing opportunity to exercise good self-care habits (McMinn et al. 2005). Spending time with God is a must for clergymen. The work of ministry is walking in the assignment wherein they have been called, and understanding and fulfilling God's work is the ultimate purpose of the call of ministry.

Family care is another vital source of self-care. Family is everything for having good and fulfilling ministries. Good relationships with wives and children make serving meaningful and relational. It is good to have a healthy outlet to release some of the strain and stress in ministry. Having a spouse who is understanding, considerate, and provides a covering in prayer for a spouse makes a huge difference.

Pastors need to utilize the various resources to care for themselves and their colleagues amid all the challenging work they face (McMinn et al. 2005). Healthy marriages, healthy families, and a good time to connect with good people are needed. Friendships, mentoring, and accountability relationships are very important for pastors. Unfortunately, many fail to recognize these resources as primary coping resources (McMinn et al. 2005).

A New England study revealed how some pastors fail to care for themselves. "We give ourselves to other people listening to their hurts, mending their wounds-yet fail to care for ourselves. Many spiritual leaders are like hosts who run around catering to the needs of their guests" (Vaccarino 2013, 69).

Pastoral Responsibility

The role of the pastor comes with great responsibility. The work entailed in this field must be executed with a clear understanding of what comes along with the role. There is something known as ministry satisfaction. "A minister's job satisfaction or dissatisfaction is largely an artifact of his relative ability to fulfill the roles and perform the functions of the ministry as he perceives it" (Powell 2009, 235). Pastors have a highly visible leadership role (Rowold 2008). Transformational leaders can inspire followers to go beyond their expected levels of commitment and contribution (Rowold 2008).

This comes through the leaders' modeling of task-related values and the commitment the leaders have toward their organization (Rowold 2008). It is with this style of leadership leaders are inspired to keep excelling and climbing for greater identifiable results.

There are pastors in ministry who have found a way to earn the title of long tenured. A long-tenured pastorate is essential for cultivating congregational vitality. It is noteworthy to have a responsible and clear dialogue of what characteristics bring about a long-standing and successful ministry (Strunk, Milacci, and Zabloski 2017). These themes were identified in extensive research (Burns et al.): spiritual formation, self-care, and emotional and cultural intelligence.

The heart of ministry is being the go-to, come-to caregiver of the souls of men and women. The attitude and approach needed for those who follow a leader must be shown, proven, and modeled by having a secure and strong relationship on a day-to-day basis. It is essential and implied by scripture verses that to be a good shepherd or pastor, one must have good relationships (Adiprasetya 2018). A reflective scripture reads, "To whom much is given much is required" (Luke 12:48 KJV). Lay leaders look to pastors as leaders; therefore, the weight and responsibility placed on them requires them to rely on them, be open to feedback, have their best interest at heart, and be involved for the people they lead (Puls, Ludden, and Freemyer 2014). "In today's Christian community pastors are responsible for spiritual guidance and development, motivation, restoration, care, correction, protection, unity, and encouragement of parishioners (and) many are responsible for the organizational development of the church" (Puls, Ludden, and Freemyer). Every leader and shepherd should have courage. Courage is the trait revealed when faced with danger or pain (Resane 2014). This kind of leadership depicts boldness, confidence, and absolute bravery (Resane 2014). There is a noteworthy quality that goes along with a gifted, talented, and anointed leader; it is called charisma. "Charisma must be attributed to a leader by followers" (Corcoran and Wellman 2016, 310–311).

The charisma comes through in a leader's speech, gestures, dress style, and the posture he or she has when standing behind the sacred desk and when engaged in teaching and ministering the Word.

Success in Ministry

There must be more to success in ministry than having just executive power as a leader. A power known as referent is observed in ministry. It is the attraction and influence that is inherent in every leader (Heinrichs 1993). Gaining this kind of power comes from respect and a likeness of the personality of lay leaders. Leaders have to have the mind to develop and grow into who they strive to become. That requires self-discipline, dedication, and focus. There needs to be more research in the area of leadership development and more focus on the growth and strength of individual leaders to be progressive (Sparkman 2018). Successful pastoral ministry has many sectors that must come through in the style and manner a pastor chooses to display. Relational leadership brings about influence from the vein that is built on personal trust (Young and Firmin 2014). Trust must be earned. "Relating to people is important, they have to see you as a real person, and you have to speak to them in their real-world" (Young and Firmin 2014, 5). The research reveals emotional intelligence has a strong connection and relationship to successful leadership skills (West 2016). Emotional intelligence is part of the growth and maturity of the leader serving and ministering in the role they are called to serve. It is a rich dividend for anyone who pursues the discipline of leadership throughout the life span and professional career of pastoral care (West 2016).

Effectiveness in Ministry

It is a secure pastor who will admit he or she does not know everything. Effective ministers are not afraid but willingly seek help in areas they are not as skillful and knowledgeable in. Acknowledging this area of their lives demonstrates they can learn other things in time (McKenna, Yost, and Boyd 2007). Secondly, pastors are forever learning. The experiences many pastors encounter happen in the day-to-day engagement and involvement in the ministry. Pressure brings out the best in a pastor, developing their resolve as situations present themselves (McKenna, Boyd, and Yost 2007).

Research focuses on the ingredient and the method that keeps a leader relevant and in touch with the work of ministry. The pulse of a ministry has many things going on at one time, and a leader who is attentive to his or her surroundings knows the best practices to keep moving along well without missing a beat. Enforcing a good self-care practice is job one. To have a sustainable workplace and a satisfying place of ministry, there needs to be some attention to minimize burnout; therefore, self-care is an adequate system of support in a minister's professional role and personal life (Bledsoe and Sutterlund 2015). Some of the strategies here include physical health activities, proper rest, adjusting flexible schedules, establishing healthy boundaries, and counsel when facing challenges in the ministry (Bledsoe and Sutterlund 2015). "Self-care represents a fundamental aspect of long-term success in professional ministry that protects against negative health outcomes such as obesity" (Bledsoe and Sutterlund 2015, 49). As Christian counselors in the pastoral field, the scriptures support being in health and prospering well. It is a successful and wise pastor who maintains good emotional health practices and takes advantage of the support systems, including congregational support (Bledso and Sutterlund 2015).

Several key factors support the theory of thriving and doing well in ministry. These areas are the motivation to serve God, job satisfaction, and psychological, physical, and spiritual well-being (Bledsoe and Sutterlund 2015). An explanation of thriving in ministry follows: "Clergy who thrive are those who have obtained success or prosperity throughout their careers through a variety of factors that may include a consistent desire to serve God and lead his people, the ability to reflect upon and learn from important experiences in ministry, and a focus on maintaining self-care and adequate support systems" (Bledsoe and Sutterlund 2015, 50).

The State of the Church

The state of affairs of a healthy church is crucial for its well-being. A healthy church functions well in the body of Christ, and the people who attend are unified with Christ and in agreement with one another as a community of faith, at the same time pursing the will of God (Manala 2010). This is carried out by four key elements: good doctrine, holistic relationships, biblically appropriate roles, and walking in vibrant growth with God and others (Manala 2010).

Every pastor wants the house he builds to be a place of love, unity, and strength. Strong leadership, prudent management, and dedicated and committed services are necessary for the house of God to remain the living organism, the life-giving body of Christ (Manala 2010). The biblical servant Nehemiah exemplifies a servant leader with a strong acumen, a dynamic leader (Manala 2010). The roles Nehemiah executed, such as bringing the workers to see the worth and responsibility of the operation of building the wall, delegating authority, and appointing the right leaders and workers to come alongside him, made everyone motivated with the right enthusiasm to accomplish this work for the glory of God (Manala 2010).

Leadership in Ministry

Leadership takes the right person, with the right plan, with the right focus to move people to an expected outcome. People want to follow a leader with a vision, a leader who knows how to get from point A to point B. It takes fortitude, clear focus, and energy for one to stay motivated and with the mindset to win. There is a symbolism that has to be saturated in the body of Christ that everyone concerned needs to recognize. "Christ is, according to the Bible, the only head of the church identified with the body of Christ. This identification suggests that the church is a living system or organism" (Manala 2010, 2). This mindset directs the members to see the value of the place they serve and how well it provides leadership and direction. The pastor then likens to this as a major symbol in the church system; he or she directs the body to Christ, and the work of ministry is done with excellence (Manala 2010).

Ministry requires working alongside people to help the growth and success of the ministry. It cannot be a one-man show. The moment it becomes about a personality, the organization will lose its strength, burnout will creep in, and there will be a real problem. There is what is known as a sharing function, as pastors need to keep moving on the path of excellence and on the road of endurance. First, sharing narcissism, giving up of the self, of wanting to share the center stage and be the only one who gets the credit. There has to be a place for everyone to feel important and necessary so that a pastor does not get all the credit. Second, sharing of responsibility. If a pastor holds all the responsibilities, the members will not act responsibly. Third, all pastors must share authority—not all but some. When an individual in a ministry is given responsibility, there must be a layer of authority along with it. Last, as the visionary and leader of the ministry, the pastor must share control (Manala 2010). In all of these roles of including others, one must not forget an important aspect of ministry. The pastor must always share the God-given vision. This draws the body in with the leader to keep the momentum and excitement (Manala 2010). "Leaders inspire a shared vision. They envision the future, and they enlist others in a common vision" (Manala 2010, 2).

Leadership transitions bring about adjustments and settling when people in leadership roles step down or rise up. Data was constructed for analysis of leadership transitions from a 2006–2007 cross-sectional component that determined how new leadership affected the relationship with members of a congregation. Conflict and membership decline were revealed in this study (Dollhopf and Scheitle 2013). Consequently, if the conflict becomes strong enough, it is inevitable that a change of leadership will follow (Dollhopf and Scheitle 2013). Conflict can be both cause and effect of congregational leadership changes (Dollhopf and Scheitle).

Further research would help determine how the long-term and short-term consequences affect the leadership transition of a congregation as well as the leadership (Dollhopf and Scheitle 2013).

Grit

Leaders with the fortitude to take others along with them who follow and support them in ministry have grit—the ability to grow, expand, and persevere in the work of ministry. Psychologist Dr. Carol Dweck states, "In a fixed mindset, people believe their basic qualities, like their intelligence or talent, are simply fixed traits" (Borling and Laselle 2018, 35). "Thus, in a growth mindset, we would believe that we are in control of our abilities, talents, and habits. We would understand that throughout life we can choose to develop and grow and to accomplish anything we want" (Borling and LaSalle 2018, 35). There are no limitations for pastors to make their ministries flourish, expand, and grow, and the people will see and feel the interest and dedication needed to make a difference in the lives of the followers. "In many ways, pastors are already some of the most resilient humans on the planet" (Barna 2017, 156).

Spirituality

The spirituality of resilience is revealed by the prophet Jeremiah as he speaks about a tree near a stream that recovers from the harshness of the heat or drought. "They will be like a tree planted by the water that sends out its roots by the stream. It does not fear when heat comes; its leaves are always green" (Jeremiah 17:8 NIV).

Like resilience, a tree grows despite the stress that surrounds it, and the growth represents trusted relationships that are like roots near the stream, causing the tree to grow in a dry place (Doehring 2015). Resilient persons, families, and organizations grow under hardship and other stress-related factors because they are deeply rooted and surrounded by life-giving relationships (Doehring 2015). Every pastor should be surrounded by a stream that flows and brings about growth in the work of ministry. Even in the dry places, there must be a sense of resilience to not allow anything to stop the flow of ministry.

There are candidates for ministry who can begin a congregation and expand and grow congregations, and it is candidates like this who have the potential to build ministries (Mattes 2017). Pastors like this are resilient. When opposition and stress occur, these men do not flee or fight back with abuse, but rather they will bear all things, hope all things, and endure all things (Mattes 2017). Paul in the New Testament exemplified resilient leadership, revealing it is obtained through the power of the Holy Spirit, which comes through afflictions, hardships, and calamities (Forney 2010)

Education for Resiliency

During the crisis with Hurricane Katrina, a Resilience Education Intervention program was developed to help pastors overcome the impact the trauma had on their communities (Abernethy, Grannum, Gordon, Williams, and Currier 2016). Researchers have determined the appropriate and effective measures for pastors and other ministry professionals are necessary for strengthening the psychological needs and mitigating burnout and other issues that affect communities after a serious disaster takes place or other traumatic events (Abernethy et al. 2016). One of the key benefits of this program is that, from an educational perspective, it helped prevent burnout. The program aimed to promote physical, emotional, spiritual, and relational aspects of healthy living to encourage and help pastors who were affected by the disaster (Abernethy et al.).

The Bible is a great resource for pulling out the power of resilience through the scriptures. It is a pastoral mandate to ensure people read the Bible with a great sense of vigor and excitement, which will help them grow in their faith and give them the strength when a crisis comes (Carson 2019).

Clergy Wellness in Ministry

One cannot escape the seriousness of measuring the spiritual well-being of the clergy. The focus of this population has attention on two constructs: spirituality and religiosity (Proeschold-Bell, Yang, Toth, Rivers, and Carder 2014).

Physical and mental health, well-being, work-related behavior, and religious spirituality are all important to bring balance and discipling to the life of clergymen. The emotional strains and pressures on these men and women are not myths; they are factual indeed (Voltmer, Thomas, and Spahn 2011).

The work of clergymen keeps them moving at a fast and at times hectic pace. The clergy vocation is unique in its diverse range of professional responsibilities (Lindholm, Johnston, Dong, Moore, and Ablah 2014, 98). Research shows they are exposed to a lifestyle that is hectic, fragmented, and emotionally challenging, in addition to having little structure or predictability (Lindholm, Johnston, Dong, Moore, and Ablah 2014, 98). It is necessary for pastors to be fit and maintain a healthy lifestyle, in adherence to the words of Paul, "Beloved, I wish above all things that thou mayest prosper and be in health, even as thy soul prospereth" (3 John 2 KJV).

It is important to note pastors are the front-line leaders as it pertains to men and women in a ministry seeking help. Having an awareness of mental health issues is a valuable asset. Lay counseling is a practice many ministries have focused on in their churches.

Lay Christian counseling for general psychological, emotional, and relational problems is an important ministry in the local church and other parachurch contexts (Clinton and Pingleton 2017, 120). Scrutiny of the duties of pastors in Australia has come into play, questioning whether counseling is the role of pastors in this region (Beaumont 2011). In the US, pastoral counseling has emerged into a specialized and interdisciplinary field with highly skilled practitioners (Beaumont 2011, 119). The reality of it is lay counseling in the United States is a viable option for persons with mental and relational needs (Clinton and Pingleton 2017, 121).

Leading the charge in ministry requires sound and solid leadership. In a changing and evolving world, it requires leaders adapting new ideas and creative means of gaining the attention of pastors to adopt a healthy attitude in serving in ministry. The spiritual understanding of clergymen being well and whole introduced an interesting concept in a recent study in the UK. Jones discovered the work of Foucault's concept of pastoral power draws on Christian writings, particularly the biblical metaphor of the shepherd and the Christian practice of confession (Jones 2018, 990). The shepherd guides the moral conduct of its followers, and the confession allows them to examine their way of living (Jones 2018). Pastors need to have an honest and healthy outlook on how they manage ministry and their personal self-care. Moral failure will bring about health decline issues in ministry (Foy and Muller 2018).

Many clergies felt the lack of space needed for themselves and were considered always in ministry. This leads to burnout (Fallon, Rice, and Howie 2013). It is a known fact that ministers are susceptible to depression. Further study is needed to see if there is a correlation to narcissistic behavior disorder (Capps 2014).

Burnout of Ministry

A study was conducted to assess the quality of life of pastors, to reveal high levels of stress, burnout, and depression. It is important to understand the work of a pastor is more than anyone can expect, and before an individual accepts the call, make sure the calling is of a surety to avoid disaster or disappointment (Staley, McMinn, Gathercoal, and Free 2013).

A humanistic approach was conducted in exposing the items that can cause burnout in ministry: social network circles, relational capacity, and the effectiveness of one's ministry. Stress has become more prominent among leaders, and many are finding themselves burned out from their day-to-day involvement (Pickett, Barrett, Eriksson, and Kabiri 2017).

It is suggested many pastors and clergymen experience and encounter severe burnout and depersonalization from their jobs, contributing to the high levels of pressure they face in addition to the workload and roles of confusion that they experience periodically (Snelgar, Renard, and Shelton 2017).

Burnout is described as the process of physical, emotional, and mental exhaustion triggered by depletion of the ability to cope with one's day-to-day environment; caused by frustration, powerlessness, and the inability to reach one's goals (Louw 2105). It is further expanded to develop as a construct to measure job-related stress for individuals who are involved in "people work" (Rodgerson and Piedmont 1998). Despite thirty years of research, burnout is still prevalent in the field of this vocation (Beebe 2007).

An Osmer's heuristic approach was conducted to highlight the pros and cons of why pastors are leaving the ministry. North American pastors who do not know how to deal with adversity and lack the means or tools to help them navigate the waters that are filled with problems need some strong processes in place (Elkington 2013).

It was discovered that a negative interpretation of personal criticism along with family criticism caused a significant drop in a minister's sense of well-being. Additionally, the greater the supportive relationships, the greater the well-being of the congregation (Doolittle 2010).

Ministry alone is one of the most fulfilling and pleasurable experiences in the lives of pastors. The research reveals "though parish ministry at its best can be wonderfully fulfilling for clergy, it can also be tough and demanding, and there is frequently the lurking danger of burnout" (Randall 2013, 333). Jared Pingleton writes, "As with most things in life, prevention is easier and better than cure. He further examines the means wherein to avoid the anguish of burnout. One must recognize the classic indicators of burnout" (*The Care and Counsel Bible* 2001, 919).

The demands placed upon pastors bring about burnout from three dimensions, according to the research study: emotional exhaustion, depersonalization, and reduced accomplishment (Chandler 2009, 273). This research was conducted from a survey of 270 pastors. Failure to replenish all that a pastor gives in serving brings on other issues that causes depletion, such as inordinate time demands, unrealistic expectations, sense of inadequacy, fear of failure, loneliness, and spiritual dryness (Chandler 2009, 274).

A UCLA Loneliness Scale was used to assess the loneliness status of clergymen in rural communities. Based on their current circumstances, it was predicted to reveal a state of loneliness while serving in these ministries (Scott and Lovell 2015). There are a myriad of tasks conducted by these pastors, to run the church in all of its capacities, beginning with the sacredness, the dull, even functioning in areas of ministry they are not trained to do (Scott and Lovell 2015). Research has repeatedly shown that the pastoral profession can be emotionally taxing (Scott and Lovell 2015, 72).

The research exposed the fact that weak internal orientation was associated with higher depression, anxiety, emotional exhaustion, depersonalization, and a lowered sense of personal accomplishment (Miner, Sterland, and Dowson 2009, 475). This results from the dependence on insufficient, precarious internal supports or fickle external supports, rather than on more stable inner spiritual or personal convictions to guide their response to existential concerns (Miner, Sterland, and Dowson 2009, 466).

This study highlighted variables that were predictive of clergy satisfaction and emotional exhaustion, which are two distinct parts of burnout (Adams, Hough, Preschool-Bell, Yao, and Kolkin 2017). Having the right tools in place, mindfulness and spirituality, will help prevent burnout from taking place in ministry (Frederick, Dunbar, and Thai 2018).

There are various ages of men in women serving in the vocation of ministry. Burnout and depression have both related to age and level of experience of clergy in addition to long-term patterns in various ways (Muse, Love, and Christensen 2016). The relationships of ministry has a great impact on the lives of those serving. Further issues such as stress can add to the complexity of the job if not rightfully balanced and managed (Wells, Probst, McKeown, Mitchem, and Whitening 2012).

Research has revealed numerous common stressors and challenges that affect clergymen and their families. There have been few studies as to how stress has an interactional effect with spouses of clergymen (Cattich 2012).

Having in place protection of the physical and emotional health of clergymen, the welfare of their families, and the safety and movement of their congregations, and having a clear and direct understanding of occupational stress and burnout is essential (Visker, Rider, and Humprhres-Ginther 2017).

Long-term engagement is associated with burnout that takes place in daily stresses in the workplace that can have a cumulative effect on a worker's emotional state (Helms, Cheshire, and Walters 2015).

Stress is more commonly exposed in younger pastors than pastors who are more experienced. Age alone was the biggest predictor in the model used with the questionnaires in a survey (Cafeteria 2017). A quantitative and qualitative assessment was conducted with seventy-three men and women of their stress levels in ministry. One of the means was a questionnaire that consisted of open-ended questions to help make the best possible assessment of their responses to this study (Berry, Francis, Rolph, and Rolph 2011).

The church as we know it will always have its crises. A church that does not experience a crisis is quite the opposite of what is read in the New Testament church in the Bible (Dryer 2015). Paul is one of the greatest scholars of the New Testament and testifies of this very sentiment when he writes, "We are hard-pressed on every side, yet not crushed; we are perplexed, but not in despair; persecuted, but not forsaken; struck down, but not destroyed; always carrying about in the body the dying of the Lord Jesus, that the life of Jesus also may be manifested in our mortal flesh. So then death is working in us, but life in you" (2 Corinthians 4:8–12 NKJV).

Using the Attachment God Inventory as a tool to note the maturity and growth of those in ministry appears to be a worthwhile investment (Cooper, Bruce, Harman, and Boccaccini 2009). Individuals who had a secure attachment style were more theologically tolerant of the Christian faiths different from their own. This brought about more peace and less distress in their spiritual lives (Cooper, Bruce, Harman, and Boccaccian 2009).

Christian Counseling

There has been a great deal of research to determine how psychologists cope with stress and maintaining their well-being. The study has not found much research in determining how clergy can function and maintain any level of resiliency and personal ethics in the demanding work of pastors (Meek, McMinn, Brower, Burnett, McRay, Ramey, and Swanson 2003).

The vision of a ministry can encounter an unexpected failure when the results of a ministry do not achieve the intended or projected results. This brings a sense of ineffectiveness and lack of accomplishment by the clergyman at the helm of ministry.

Gaps

The gaps in this research have many that address the reason some pastors stay, why some leave, and what a good mindset is for pastors to become long-tenured men and women of God serving in ministry. Several factors contribute to the keys of a successful pastor, including self-care, mental health, and spiritual well-being.

Research has been conducted to determine why pastors walk away from ministry. The study is revealing due to the various reasons one chooses to step away. Most who walk away do not return to any form of ministry in the church. The most common reason in many instances is the lack of preparation (Stewart 2009). This is just the beginning of one of many reasons to be revealed and discovered.

3

METHODS

Overview

The research to explore the vocational work of men and women in ministry takes on an investigation to expose the findings and issues that have caused an alarming exodus of clergymen walking away from their assignments. It is estimated more than two hundred and fifty pastors walk away from ministry every month (Pastoral Care, Inc. 2020). This is not just your everyday nine-to-five job; it is a profession where many say there was a divine calling, longing, and passion to commit their lives in the works of ministry to serve, minister, and help those in need of pastoral care. As the research opens the doors to issues such as pastors in ministry, stressful encounters, training to enhance ministry, burnout, leadership, termination, and the like, what appears is a deep and concerning need for clergymen to seek help themselves. Ministry is a calling; many are called, but only a few are chosen.

Design

Phenomenological research is a qualitative research method that was originally designed by Edmund Husserl. This design was fashioned or tailored to provide psychological researchers in the investigation of a human lived experience and behavior (Wertz 2005).

Four processes will take place in the research of this design. First, epoch, preparation for deriving new knowledge but also as an experience in itself; a process of setting aside predilections, prejudices, predispositions, and allowing things, events, and people to enter anew into consciousness and look and see them again, as if for the first time (Moustakas 1994, 85). Second, phenomenological reduction, the task of describing in a textural language just what one sees, not only in terms of the external object but also the internal act of consciousness, the experience as such, the rhythm and relationship between phenomenon and self (Moustakas 1994, 90). Third, imaginative variation to seek possible meanings through the utilization of imagination, varying the frames of reference, employing polarities and reversals, and approaching the phenomenon from divergent perspectives, different positions, roles, or functions (Moustakas 1994, 97–98). The last is synthesis of meanings and essences, the intuitive integration of the fundamental textural and structural descriptions into a unified statement of the essences of the experience of the phenomenon (Moustakas 1994, 100).

These four factors (epoch, phenomenological reduction, imaginative variation, and synthesis) are essential to conduct phenomenological research (Moustakas 1994, 101). Phenomenology does not form theories, operationalize variables, deduce or test hypotheses, or use probabilistic calculations to establish confidence, as do positivist and neopositivist approaches (Wertz 2005, 175).

Lastly, Max Van Manen states, measures such as content validity, criterion-related validity, and construct validity apply to tests, and measures are not compatible with phenomenological methodology (Manen 2014, 347).

Meaning and Method

There are two types of designs to approach this proposal. The first is the hermeneutic phenomenology, a method of abstemious reflection on the basic structures of the lived experience of human existence (Manen 2016, 26).

The second style is the transcendental. This approach engages in disciplined and systematic efforts to set aside prejudgments regarding the phenomenon being investigated to launch the study as far as possible, free of preconceptions, beliefs, and knowledge of the phenomenon from prior experience and professional studies—to be completely open, receptive, and naive in listening to and hearing research participants describe their experience of the phenomenon being investigated (Moustakas 1994, 22). The transcendental design is the approach used for the lived experiences of the pastors in the Church of God in Christ.

The research design selected is a phenomenology design. Moustakas says, "Phenomenology is rooted in questions that give a direction and focus to meaning, and in themes that sustain an inquiry, awaken further interest and concern, and account for our passionate involvement with whatever is experienced" (1994, 59). The lived experience is a true depiction of this type of research that provides the researcher a hands-on approach and in real-life, real-world presence to share the story of the participants involved.

The proposed participants would involve the selection of senior pastors who have served in ministry successfully. Secondly, these senior pastors are from a common denominator or circle of influence so that the stories are relatable, complementary, and reflective of the lifestyles, ministry approach, and engagement of each in serving their various congregations. Phenomenology asks, "What is this or that kind of experience like?" (Manen 1997, 9). The various experiences a senior pastor has will convey the triumphs and moments that highlight what the experiences they encountered felt like and what kind they may have been. It differs from almost every other science in that it attempts to gain insightful descriptions for the way we experience the world prereflectively, without taxonomizing, classifying, or abstracting it (Manen 1997, 9).

This leads to the focus of this research study. The research will center upon having a narrative, descriptive discussion about a question that will hopefully further the research of understanding of the resilience, fortitude, and tenacity of those who have remained faithful and committed to their ministries with great success. An Osmer's heuristic approach was conducted to highlight the pros and cons of why pastors are leaving the ministry. It further precludes North American pastors who do not know how to deal with adversity; therefore, the lack of a means or tool to help them navigate the waters filled with problems require some strong processes in place (Elkington 2013).

Survey/Interview Questions

Table 2 presents the survey/interview questions used in the collection of the research data.

Table 2. Survey/interview questions

Question 1.   What made you have the assurance you were called by God for ministry?

Question 2.   How has education affected your calling as a pastor?

Question 3.   What sparked the passion in you to enter into ministry and seek the role of senior pastor?

Question 4.   How do you define success in ministry and as a professional?

Question 5.   Why is being ordained important to you in ministry?

Question 6.   What are the signs of ministry that provoked you to be successful?

Question 7.   What infrastructures did you put in place to help you stay the task in ministry both naturally and spiritually?

Question 8.   How important is it to establish an inner circle of other pastors in your circle of ministry?

Question 9.   What preparations have you made for serving in the role of a senior pastor?

Question 10.   How did you navigate challenging moments in your ministry?

Question 11.   How important is family life for you as a pastor?

Question 12.   How necessary are finances to establishing ministry?

From the research to date, more work needs to be accomplished. The research question guides an investigation and must be carefully constructed, every word deliberately chosen and ordered in such a way that the primary words appear immediately, capture attention, and guide the phenomenological process of seeing, reflecting, and knowing (Moustakas 1994, 59)

Ministry is a work that requires true commitment and dedication to the work of service. "Let the elders that rule well be counted worthy of double honor, especially they who labor in the word and doctrine" (1 Timothy 5:17 KJV). A senior pastor has labored untiringly. He or she has given of themselves, their families, and their lives for the call they surrendered to for God.

Participants and Setting

The participants, as stated briefly in this proposal, will comprise of pastors who have served in ministries in the Church of God in

Christ across the nation in various states. The pastors are the senior leaders of the various ministries who have served in ministry for ten years or more. The pool I will work with will come from the ecclesiastical offices in ministry. The pool of pastors will include seven to ten men who appear to be on the cutting edge of ministry, looking on the outside, not knowing how the churches operate on a day-to-day basis. These are African American pastors, and while Caucasians are also serving in the Church of God in Christ, it is a predominately African American denomination. The ages will vary from forty years to seventy-five. Most pastors serving in the church are married men, husbands with children, which will provide some insight into the family dynamics of this research.

My approach will be to prepare letters and send them to churches whose pastor in the Church of God in Christ has dedicated their lives to the ministry and ask if they would be willing to be a coresearcher in this endeavor. The letter would also include a Participant Release Agreement to further document the entire process. After the letters are signed and acknowledged, the research would be conducted. And after it is completed, a formal thank-you letter to each coresearcher will be sent.

Upon completion of the contact, I would then explore setting up personal times to speak with each of the participants in a comfortable setting and record the conversations verbatim to ensure 100 percent accuracy of their lived experiences.

Some interviews may require travel, requiring logistical arrangements to speak with participants. Whatever means is necessary to make this lived experience informative and personal will be done to conduct these types of narratives. Manen asked the question. "What is 'lived experience'?" (Manen 1997, 35). Most lived experiences have an impact on our current reflective consciousness of our present life, our self-awareness that brings to surface our awareness, unaware of what is taking place (Manen 1997).

Instrumentation

The instrumentation used for this research are the interviews conducted between seven to ten senior pastors who have committed their lives to the ministries they have been appointed to serve in the Church of God in Christ. There will be a recording device to record the conversations. The instrument will be safeguarded and the conversations protected. Confidentiality will be at the helm, and the participants can be assured their information is shared in a safe place.

The procedure for the research through a phenomenology study is to produce a thorough, complete, exhaustive description of the phenomena of the daily living experience, including understanding the important structures of the situation itself (Heppner, Wamplod, Owen, Thompson, and Wang 2016). Interviews will be conducted, and the narratives will be written upon approval from the IRB. I intend to write letters to the participants for their engagement and support of this research study. The demographics will be in areas across the country. The Church of God in Christ has only male pastors. The age limits will vary, educational backgrounds will differ, and financial statuses will vary.

The following guidelines will be incorporated through this research: (a) philosophical perspectives and epoche, (b) research questions and lived experiences, (c) criterion-based sampling, (d) phenomenological data analysis, and (e) essential, invariant structure (or essence) of the lived experience (Heppner et al.).

Procedures

After the approval from the Institutional Review Board, the research for this study will begin. The participants will be notified through official correspondence by email, letter, to their various locations. In the interim, I will conduct a pretest of the questions with pastors connected to the Church of God in Christ while waiting for the approval to move forward with the research. The seven to ten pastors who have been identified will begin the process of being interviewed with a recording device to ensure all words, comments, and information are noted. There will be travel involved to reach each participant, as they may be spread across various demographic areas.

After obtaining informed consent, all participants will be asked the same ten to twelve questions for the research. The information gathered will support the gap of the research on pastors serving in the Church of God in Christ, with all expectations this research will provide essential, beneficial, and relevant information to help any future and present pastors serving in this denomination.

The Researcher's Personal Influence

Phenomenology is designed to eliminate any prejudgment and presuppositions, coming to a transcendent state of freshness and openness, with nothing unclear, not surrounded by customs and practices conducted, beliefs, and prejudices of normal science, which is by the habits of the way things have been seen in the world or by knowledge based on unelected everyday experience (Moustakas 1994). On this note, therefore, the biographical background of my involvement in this subject comes from a person who has been in the church all my life. I have witnessed the work of men in ministry and how they conduct, lead, serve, and balance their myriad of duties to fulfill their God-given calling. I served in the role of administrator, coordinating schedules, managing capital campaigns for fundraising, teaching, instructing, providing musical support, and preaching. "Reflection on the influence of self not only creates personal awareness of how the research is shaped by one's own biography but also provides a context within which audiences can more fully understand the researcher's interpretation of text data"

(Sword 1999, 270). In 2004, I was appointed as pastor of Faith Deliverance Church of God in Christ. The founder is an aged man who led this ministry faithfully, honorably, and in true holiness. He modeled the right behavior before me, which gave me a sound foundation to follow. "Similarly, encourage the young men to be self-controlled. In everything set them an example by doing what is good. In your teaching show integrity, seriousness, and soundness of speech that cannot be condemned, so that those who oppose you may be ashamed because they have nothing bad to say about us" (Titus 2:6–8 NIV). The changing of the guard gave me a very personal encounter and love to serve in the work as a pastor, one of the fivefold gifts of ministry. The only church background I have ever lived is with what is called the grand old Church of God in Christ. It has a rich slogan: "You can't join in, you have to be born in" (Church of God in Christ).

I began my academic journey in psychology with a secular school for nine months and then made a transition to attend a Christian college. The Christian college helped shape my worldview and my self-awareness of engaging with people from all walks of life. I have a focus in pastoral counseling. Therefore, my views and opinions are not biased or prejudiced after being exposed to the knowledge of this vocation from both sides—those who serve successfully and those who have become burned out.

Data Analysis

The document analysis will be minutes written verbatim from the notes of the conversation with each participant. The notes or minutes will be written with close and personal information, professional information, and all references of the tools and means each pastor uses to perform their role in ministry. Also, tape recordings of the conversations will be used to transcribe intricate details to ensure all points are noted, written, and shared in the research. Once all recordings are completed and notes and information are transcribed, the participants will be allowed to ensure all information was shared and if there are any final thoughts.

There are two types of designs to approach this proposal. The first is the hermeneutic phenomenology. It is a method of abstemious reflection on the basic structures of the lived experience of human existence (Manen 1997, 26). The second style is the transcendental. This approach engages in disciplined and systematic efforts to set aside prejudgments regarding the phenomenon being investigated to launch the study as far as possible, free of preconceptions, beliefs, and knowledge of the phenomenon from prior experience and professional studies—to be completely open, receptive, and naive in listening to and hearing research participants describe their experience of the phenomenon being investigated (Moustakas 1994, 22).

Summary

The investigation of the resilience and success of African American pastors serving in the Church of God in Christ is the focus of this research. With so many pastors who have chosen to walk away, it is refreshing and rewarding to learn there are pastors excited, motivated, and ready to serve in the ministry they have been called to and that the role of a pastor is worth fighting for.

The senior pastor in the Church of God in Christ holds a level of great importance and ranking among his clergymen. All pastors are selected from a pool of elders who have been ordained in their perspective offices, and when a ministry needs a pastor to be appointed, it is among these men that a level of promotion, responsibility, and availability is made.

4

FINDINGS

Overview

This chapter provides the results of the data obtained from the participants for the phenomenological study of the pastors from the Church of God in Christ. Bishop Charles Blake, the presiding bishop of the churches of God in Christ, shared these words on the leadership of a pastor who stands tall in the ranks of clergymen in this great church: "It is rare that you find people who possess uncanny business acumen, impeccable leadership, and a charismatic personality with a spirit of humility and hunger" (Dillard 2015, 4). The conversations and interviews with these men reflect these sentiments for me during this process.

There are seven men who serve as senior pastors who have taken the reins of their ministry to heart to become successful and faithful to God, leading the flock of God with diligence and an undying commitment to please God. The pastors are leading the charge in various states across the country, including Ohio, North Carolina, Wisconsin, and Tennessee. It is a good representation from the four corners of the world as the churches of God in Christ are in more than 107 countries. Their ages range from forty-two to seventy-two years. They each have served more than ten years in ministry. In the words of Herbert Davis, "Every Christian Leader should desire to build something great, something transformative, and something lasting" (Davis 2015, 30). Lasting has been the drive, tenacity, grit, and resilience of these men to faithfully and honorably serve the churches they each have been called to lead.

The essence and research for this study are based on the transcendental phenomenological study to investigate the lived experiences of the resilience and success of African American pastors serving the Church of God in Christ. This research investigation was framed around three research questions:

1. What is it about a ministry that gave some pastors the resilience and tenacity to become a long-tenured pastor?
2. What gave some pastors the strength and ability to work through difficulty that earned them the title of senior pastor?
3. What are the innate talents or abilities possessed by some pastors and implemented in their ministry that enabled a long-term tenure?

This chapter of the research will reveal the information and data collected that will provide candid and in-depth responses from the day-to-day lived experiences in their role and assignment as senior pastors.

Participants

The participants are a selected group of senior pastors serving in the Pentecostal denomination in the Church of God in Christ, Incorporated. These men have served in ministry for at least ten years. Each has served faithfully and in good standing under the organizational infrastructure and governance of the leadership of a church of more than six million men and women across the globe. These pastors shared their lived experiences as senior pastors leading the congregations they are called to serve. The participants range from forty-two to seventy years of age.

Table 3. Participants for research

Name	Age	Years in Ministry	Education Level
Participant A	62	36	High school
Participant B	72	41	Theology degree
Participant C	60	14	College
Participant D	49	24	PhD
Participant E	42	15	Master's
Participant F	55	19	Two and a half years of college
Participant G	42	19	Master of divinity

Participant A

Participant A has stood in the ranks of a shepherd for thirty-six years as a senior pastor. A father, husband, grandfather, and more importantly, a shepherd, who, in his own words, "I tested God, like Gideon" (interview with participant A, 2020), as he heeded the call to successfully serve in this vocation faithfully for God. At the age of sixty-two, he leads with strength and commitment to be the leader his congregation welcomes him to be.

Participant B

Participant B serves as the senior pastor of the midsized congregation he leads with more than forty years of experience. He is a loving husband, father, and grandfather who takes family to heart in the great tasking to lead a local congregation. One of the most memorable moments he shared were the words one of his daughters said to him: "'Dad, can I be a member of your church?' I'm like, 'What, you are already a member of my church.' She said, 'No, I want to be like everybody else. I want to be able to come into your office and talk to you like all the other members do'" (interview with participant B, 2020). Man, that blew me away. I mean I just, I didn't know what to say. Pastors give much of their lives to the family of God. Participant B immediately took note of his own daughter's feelings and continues to meet the needs of home first and then his church family.

Participant C

Participant C serves as the senior pastor of a congregation he has led with the oversight bestowed upon him by God for fourteen years. At sixty years of age, he has taken his assignment to heart with the diligence, commitment, and love for not only his devotion to his family but to the body of Christ he honorably leads. Participant C's passion as a senior pastor shined brightly from his own words during our conversation: "Having the passion to make a difference in someone's life, for me, there is nothing more rewarding when you hear someone say, 'You were responsible for saving my life.' And for me, that is like water on a seed. It just causes me to want to do more, take the ministry further, reach another soul" (interview with participant C, 2020).

Participant D

Participant D stands tall among the pastors interviewed during this research. At forty-nine years of age, he is a strong, courageous, hands-on leader with the community at the forefront of all he does with his work in the kingdom of God. He has led the charge as a senior pastor for twenty-four years. He is a husband and father who has earned a PhD and has an unyielding passion for education to make one better in doing the work of ministry. His own words about how education has affected his calling and work as a pastor follow: "It has challenged me, to try to learn the word better, yes it impacted my worldview, but also for me it afforded me the chance to, as I often say, to bring language and connect my passion for justice and community effort with the church" (interview with participant D, 2020).

Participant E

Participant E is the youngest senior pastor who took part in this research at the age of forty-two years. A force to be reckoned with, he is a leader who became pastor by his eagerness to work in the role as a supply pastor, which changed the course of his work to what he has become today. He is a young husband and father who is making a difference in the kingdom of God. Participant E said, "God used that opportunity to confirm for me that I was called to the pastoral ministry, because if he had not set me up for it, I would not be pastoring" (interview with participant E, 2020).

Participant F

Participant F has served as senior pastor for nineteen years with the congregation he was blessed to serve after the death of Ohio Northwest's loss of the late Bishop Robert L. Chapman. He is a husband, father, and anointed musical pastor who is gifted to preach and sing. He brought a steady conversation about his ministry during this research interview. The question was asked, "What sparked the passion in you to enter into the ministry and seek the role of senior pastor?" Participant F stated, "I want to say making a difference in Christendom with a servant's heart. My story is I succeeded a great man. And I was his heir apparently, and with that, it propelled me into the pastorship" (interview with participant F, 2020). This is a great example of how the succession of a leader is made in the Church of God in Christ during one of the most transitional moments in ministry.

Participant G

Participant G steps into the ranks of pastorship as the game changer of a generation who is looking for a leader to lead by example and take the work of ministry to heart day one on the job. At forty-two, he has climbed the ranks from pastor to the role of bishop in the Church of God in Christ. He has hit the ground running, being a father, husband, and the senior pastor who keeps on setting the precedence for greater works to come. Humility is a strong characteristic reflected in this leader. During the interview, he stated, "Having a heart of servanthood is very significant in understanding the role of a senior pastor. As we all understand, Jesus said, 'Whoever is greatest among you be the servant of all.' Accepting that role and responsibility as a pastor most definitely there must have been a heart matter" (interview with participant G, 2020).

Participants' Response by Question

Table 4 presents participants' responses by question.

Table 4. Participants' responses by question

Question 1: What made you have the assurance you were called of God for ministry?	
Participant A	The assurance for me that I was called of God for ministry came with several factors for me. I respected the confirmation of others, and in my own space, I had a vision from God. More importantly for me, I tested God, like the character of Gideon.
Participant B	Well, I think first of all to even receive a call at all you have to be saved. You first have to have some kind of personal relationship with Christ yourself. Of course, at the same time you understand the responsibility of that call in terms of preparing yourself as a disciple of Jesus Christ in the real world, not just saying it but actually living that kind of life that glorifies and exalts him, lifts him up ultimately. For me, I really didn't have a lot of personal confirmation from other people. My confirmation came from God himself. I did not want to be a minister, did not want to preach, that was not in my bloodline. Amos, said. "I was neither a prophet nor the son of a prophet" (Amos 7:14 NIV). So was my dad. In fact, my father wasn't even saved. So that was not in my thoughts or intentions. I had no real desire to do that, but I had to wrestle with God. I had to literally fight with God about ministry because I didn't want to do it. So I ultimately found myself, we were in a very high service one night, I think it might have been on a Friday night, and the spirit of the Lord was high and I found myself up in the pulpit. So that was my confirmation because I knew that was not where I wanted to be. That was a real confirmation for me. So then of course, after I entered into the ministry other people were kind of encouraging me and that kind of thing.
Participant C	I'm going to answer that all of the above. And with a footnote others, that burning desire, confirmation through others, I also, the call I heard, but I kept hearing God. That's what really triggered everything. I kept hearing from him. It's like we're talking right now, I heard him and it would manifest itself in certain ways, sometimes in a dream, sometimes through others, but I just kept hearing him, so I would say that was the deciding factor.
Participant D	It was confirmation from God. That was very much encouraged, my mother pushed that. I was trying to get her because my grandfather was a pastor, so I was trying to get her my mother to tell me something like they prophesied it when you were a kid, but she was like, "Naw, baby, you need to know for yourself." These black folks in church will try to make everybody a preacher. You have to know for yourself. It was from God.

Participant E	For me I'm going to say, first of all the environment I was raised. I grew up in a home that was Christ-centered, ministry focused, so I think I developed a appetite, and a desire for ministry early on in my life. I began ministry when I was a toddler and I think as I began to grow, becoming older I began to connect my life experiences with the call to assist people, also had experienced some of the things that myself and my family did. I felt my purpose on earth.
Participant F	I would say it was a specific vision from God. It was something I ran from, I didn't want, didn't even desire. It was absolutely God.
Participant G	I really think it may be a mixture of all of those, I don't know if that's an appropriate answer. I think if my memory serves me correctly, it mentions a confirmation by others, it says vision from God, I think that could be conclusive of you know just the leading, the prompting of the Spirit of God and a desire to please God. So I think it's probably not one of a specific answer it could be a hybrid or mixture of all of them. That really brought me to the point of understanding what the call of God was for our life.

Question 2: How has education affected your calling as a pastor?

Participant A	My educational background and training came from reading and studying God's Word and following leadership.
Participant B	You know years ago in Memphis during the last time of J.O. Patterson, the presiding bishop of the church and he made a statement that "You can't teach what you don't know and you can't lead where you don't go." That stuck with me I guess over forty years ago. That stuck with me how to really understand how relevant Christian education is if you are going to be a leader. You can never stop learning, never stop growing you will never stop developing. It is a lifetime process. Never quit. There is no goal you can reach and say, "OK I have finally arrived." That doesn't happen if you are a leader. You are constantly growing, constantly developing, constantly evolving into all that God wants you to be. So education, the more education you can get, the more effective you can be as a leader. You learn the skills, you learn how to understand the people, understand what it is that God has called you to do. So education is very important for that process. It equips you with personal skills, decision-making skills, organizational skills all of those kinds of things you are going to need if you are going to be an effective leader.

Participant C	I would say other, as for me, what education has done for me. I know that there is a calling and an anointing on my life. What that has done it has allowed it to go further, be advanced, enhanced. The anointing that God has given to me. I was thinking of a scripture where it says, God has given us the ability with the power to get wealth, he didn't particularly put wealth in our hands but I have given you resources to go get. I look at education the same way. With ministry, we can desire all these things that we want but to take it to the next level in a lot of cases you need to take what God has given us or what he has made available and use it to advance.
Participant D	I'd probably say other. Because I think it is all of those. It has challenged me, to try to learn the Word better, yes it impacted my worldview, but also for me it afforded me the chance to as I often say, to bring language, and connect my passion for justice and community effort with the church. With the purpose and call of ministry. Because I was raised in church, my parents never directedly connected their social actions, their social activism to faith. They just said, "This is the right thing to do." It was through the academy that I actually got exposed to liberation theology, black theology, feminist, womanistic theology, and learned there was language to the fact that the church called me to be involved in the community and to fight for justice, not just to jump and shout, be sanctified and in the church.
Participant E	Education, being seminary trained, really gave me a greater understanding of my call. I think it helped me to define the purpose of my assignment. And it assisted me in digging deep within myself and learning what was in me to give. It helped me to know how to execute the ministry God had given me.
Participant F	I want to say the second one, I think it has enhanced my passion. In all thy getting, get an understanding. If we are not able to rightly divide the Word of God, and we are not taught from the Word of God and how to execute it. We do ourselves a disservice. I think it's very imperative that we have education.
Participant G	Same thing again. I think all of them are very critical that as a minister and leader that we are to open up ourselves for opportunities for development, empowerment, for training, and if that is in a formal educational perspective, most definitely and I value education very significantly.

Question 3: What sparked the passion in you to enter into ministry and seek the role of the senior pastor?	
Participant A	I always felt I had a passion for ministry and as the role of a senior pastor I was committed to being a true follower of Christ, my love for souls was to see the Kingdom of God expanded. It was further important for me to make a difference in God's kingdom working and serving with a servant's heart. The final analysis for me; God would not take no for an answer.

Participant B	Well, probably all of those. Like I said earlier, I didn't want to be a preacher. I didn't feel qualified. I didn't feel like I knew enough to be a preacher because the one's I had observed were men who were educated, very refined men, and I didn't think I fit that role, I didn't fit the mode. I didn't want to go there. So God just kind of grabbed me and kind of jumped over a whole lot of other people and got to me. Threw me in the lion's den. That was not my intention. An opportunity came in the late seventy's in the life of the late Robert L. Chapman a church in Cleveland that came open. Nobody wanted to pastor that church. They had gone through five or six pastors already. Nobody wanted to take that church so he asked me. Being a young and adventurous type guy I said, "Sure, I will give it a try." So I did. Stayed there for three and half years, my wife and I commuted. One Sunday morning they gave me a letter and said, "You're fired." I thought at that time I was a failure, it wasn't going to work. I asked God to give me some direction and he did. He opened up a door that was back in 1981 and the rest is history. God has been moving every since.
Participant C	I would say, mercy, can I answer all of the above? Again, all of the above because truthfully I genuinely want to make a difference in someone's life. And as I mentioned earlier, I ran from it for a long time but I know that the anointing is on my life to make a difference. You know, anointing comes from the Hebrew word, which means to smear, and when you can make a difference when you can take what God has given you and help others with it, that just drives me, it just absolutely drives me, but again, it was that call from God that told me to do this work, I didn't want to do this for myself.
Participant D	For me, it was making a difference in Christendom. Because like I said, I felt God calling, I also saw this opportunity as I have always believed, we tried to do all these years intentionally blend Pentecostalism and social justice to me it was an opportunity to at that time I thought develop and build a church that a COGIC church I had not seen before. I have since seen them as I have learned and met more people. But at the time I thought this is going to be totally different from what I thought COGIC, of what I had been exposed to and to expand the kingdom and kind of do ministry in what I thought was a biblically faith way, different than what I was exposed to.
Participant E	Honestly, I didn't seek to be a senior pastor, I had gone to seminary and I needed a opportunity to do ministry, being that I am a part of a denomination that does not require seminary training, it also does not value seminary training like other denominations, mainline denominations and so I ended up getting an opportunity to come to Milwaukee to work and while I was here, I was offered an opportunity to be a Supply minister. Because I supplied for a church, when it was time for them to vote on their candidate, I was not one, I was requested, and as a write-in, I won the vote. God used that opportunity to really confirm for me that I was called to the pastoral ministry because if he had not set me up for it, I would not be pastoring.

Participant F	I want to say making a difference in Christendom with a servant's heart. My story is I succeeded a great man. And I was his heir apparently and with that, it propelled me into the pastorship.
Participant G	It's almost like again, a mixture, but I will say I think having a heart of servanthood is very significant in understanding the role as a senior pastor. As we all understand Jesus said, whoever is greatest among you be the servant of all. Accepting that role and responsibility as a pastor most definitely there must have been a heart matter. Notwithstanding, ultimately the call of God being convinced, convicted that this is the will of God for our lives. So being motivated by his assurance of this privilege that he has given us and then just understanding what the true call of a pastor is and aligning ourselves with that.

Question 4: How do you define success in ministry and being a professional?	
Participant A	Success in ministry is defined with four key components, fruitfulness, growth in the knowledge of Christ, making disciples of men, with the biggest factor, satisfaction in knowing that I am pleasing God.
Participant B	I was going to ask what did you mean by professional? In the sense of is it what we do as men and women what we do as a career, a vocation in life, in your craft, or being an expert in what you do? Professional development and spiritual growth is absolutely for success in ministry. You cannot be stagnant, you have to work at being all you can be and being the best you can be as it relates to leadership and that is an everyday ongoing process you are working constantly to improve who you are as a man or a woman of God. So you do whatever it is you have to do and use whatever tools you can use or make available for yourself to be the very best version of yourself that you can be. That is constant work. Success is a lot of time we think trying to reach a goal and once we reach that goal we say, "Now I'm successful." But success is not so much reaching a goal. You can climb on the top of a building but if you are on the wrong building you are not successful. Being successful is really fulfilling the assignment you have been given by God. When you fulfill that assignment then you are successful because its only at that point that God can say, "Well done, good and faithful servant."
Participant C	What I'm all about is B. Making disciples of men. That was one of the great commission, well thee great commission by Jesus Christ. A lot of times that gets lost in the shuffle of everything that's going on but ultimately that was the great commission for us to make disciples of others, I would say B.

Participant D	For me, I'd probably say other. Because of the fact I see success as fulfilling what God has called you to do and what that might look might look different based upon who you are and where you are and what you are actually called to do. I do believe it's that whole idea of expanding the kingdom, making more disciples, but I look at it as its kind of like a holistic approach so you are seeing people come to the kingdom, you're seeing people develop and grow as believers, you're seeing people hopefully moving to finding their purpose, filling their purpose and to also hopefully having some type of impact upon the community or part of the world. I don't only see ministry success is not only individualistic or in the sense of solely about numbers but also what type of impact are you having that may not necessarily be quantifiable, in the traditional aspects of doc, how many you running, what you looking at, that type of thing.
Participant E	I define success as impacting lives. I think when you have a vision you execute that vision to completion and it has impacted one or more lives I believe that's success. To me, success is completing your assignment. Whatever that is, and so, that's how I measure it. I've grown to that because at times in ministry I looked at it as what I thought it should be, what others were doing and thought I should have that, but I've learned that whatever it is that God has assigned to your hand and whoever it is he has put in your path, to influence; when you do that, you are successful.
Participant F	Do I have to pick one or can I use a couple? I would think that fruitfulness would be, that sticks in my heart, my mind, and my spirit. It's not the amount of congregants you have, it's the training, maturity, and the growth of the individuals that you serve. So I would think, making disciples those both when I heard the question that's what I was thinking. Sometimes we look at numbers and I think about the scripture that God disciplined David for numbering the people. I think we have to be careful even in this pandemic that we are not so concerned with numbers but souls.
Participant G	For me, success in ministry reflects a ministry that is fulfilling of the purpose of the assignment and the call of the ministry that God has given them. I know there is a blanket or corporate mission of the Lord's church but all of us individually as pastors and the churches we serve I believe there is a unique call that God may have for us and we find ourselves pursuing that vision and pursuing that mission and when we do that to me that's the definition of success.

Question 5: Why is being ordained important to you in ministry?	
Participant A	In the Church of God in Christ being ordained is a key role for pastors serving in ministry. It was important for me solely because of its obedience to the will of God by living a consecrated life. It is also an honor to follow the steps of the leaders who were before me who set a great example. To see the ministry I served to become successful was crucial.
Participant B	Actually, ordination really wasn't important to me. I remained a minister for seven years. The only reason I got ordained my predecessor came to me, "Don't you think it's time to be ordained?" So I said, "Well, if you think so," so I was ordained. In my mind, God had already ordained me, called me to do what he wanted me to do. Understanding our church structure there were some things I could not do unless I had ordination papers from the organization itself. So ordination in that respect was important.
Participant C	I would say, other. All those things could be or may be important, but from a natural standpoint being ordained, I think it helps doors to be opened for you, where without ordinarily without being ordained some of those doors would be shut, closed. So this is an opportunity to take the ministry further than what it can go in certain areas with other people having certain credentials.
Participant D	I probably, once again go with other, not because the options you give are all good, cause there is that sense of hierarchy, being connected to something bigger than you that I don't want to say validates or affirm but acknowledges some way, God has called you and that you know have met some standards, so that's important. I think the primary reason I say other is cause technically when I started Nehemiah, I started and was not ordained yet. So I actually started as a minister and I got ordained January, and I got ordained in the local church in July, then the jurisdiction in August. So there was a time in which, well, I'm talking too much, but anyway. There was a time in which I had that whole being ordained was man's thing didn't mean anything if God hadn't anointed you. I have since then also learned that there is value in the affirmation, and the hands being laid on, that there is a connection beyond yourself. That the ordination connects you with the tradition of your church, but also the ministry lineage that has been passed on. That is not anything to be frowned upon. Look down upon even if there were people I thought growing up were ordained and didn't demonstrate anointing, were not seemingly gifted and I thought it was better to be gifted and anointed than being ordained but as I realized it didn't have to be a bifurcation of the two, you could be anointed and gifted and ordained. There is benefit to it. A little complex answer.

Participant E	I think being ordained in the Church of God in Christ is so significant to me because it is the organization that transformed the life, the lives of my entire family. It gave me identity and to be validated within an organization that I see as family and whom taught me the tenets of my faith it's just a high honor and to have been sanctioned not only by the church, by the man who was my spiritual father who ordained me was just an invaluable experience. Secondly, I understand the necessity of ordination in order to execute fully all duties of my assignment as a clergyman.
Participant F	I'm going to say the second one. It would be the obedience to Christ. I'm Church of God in Christ through and through. I'm not going to take that away, but I don't think it's because of the organization. My allegiance is to the Lord first and then to the organization. I will probably get in trouble with that. Because my father was a Church of God in Christ pastor, my grandfather was a Church of God in Christ elder, I have uncles who were ordained in the church of God in Christ, biologically, then I served dad Chapman. It's nice to be ordained but it wasn't because of the organization it was because God had called me.
Participant G	I wish I could choose some of those options you have there but if I may go with other, I would have to say the reason ordination is important it is not exclusively from a denominational perspective but of the validation, authorization, authenticity of the call because at the end of the day it matters who lays hands on you. Ordination is not about a certificate. It is not about regalia, or the garb that one has opportunity to wear, but ordination says you have been tested, tried, vetted, and these men and leaders of great reputation and those who have been anointed themselves are sanctioning you. So you are not out there as an island, out there coming from nowhere. There is a validation of who you are. I think that goes all the way back to biblical days of the New Testament church we see in the book of Acts the scripture would say, "The Holy Ghost separated unto himself Paul and Barnabas," and yet the apostles had to come and lay hands on them. So that was somewhat of an ordination, an authorization. So that is the significance to me, even as a pastor, as a bishop, you see that the presiding bishop, general board lays hands on that bishop so it's apostolic succession and someone laid hands on this case, Bishop Charles Blake. Whoever laid hands on Bishop Charles Blake there's a link going back to Bishop Mason and we believe this link goes all the way back to Jesus Christ, so somehow and another all of us who are in the ordained ministry, in our case the Church of God in Christ should point back to Jesus Christ.

Question 6: What are the signs of ministry that provoked you to be successful?	
Participant A	I was provoked to be successful because I had the opportunity to see something small evolve into something great and I had a past, God did not hold that against me!
Participant B	My military experience. I went into the military as a minister. I met hundreds of guys who were also ministers from different parts of the country. In my mind, at the time these guys were much further ahead in the ministry than I was. Just watching them, listening to them, hearing them, some of them had been to seminary and other places of higher learning and I had none of that. Watching these young men doing what they were doing it provoked me. I said to myself, "I got to do something." So that led me to seek for greater understanding, more in-depth understanding of God's Word, and God's purpose. It then led me to buying books. At that time we really didn't have any kind of educational arm in the church, it was just developing so we didn't have a great arm at that time so we bought books, invested in my ministry because of those young men of what I had seen and heard of those young men they inspired me so it pushed me to take myself to a higher level.
Participant C	I would say again, other. And I don't want to sound like a broken record, but that passion to make a difference in someone's life for me there is nothing more rewarding when you hear someone say you were responsible for saving my life. And for me, that is like water on a seed. It just causes me to want to do more, take the ministry further, reach another soul. Go on another day regardless of whatever happens from a negative standpoint in my life when I hear, someone say listen, you made a difference in my life, that in itself produces life in me. I was talking to a bishop the other day and I told him, that to be responsible for taking someone out of darkness into the light and what God gave me was right there as we were talking, God said, "There's life in the light. There is life in the light." To be an instrument God uses literally to cause someone to live to walk in that light is just a passion.
Participant D	Wow, another other. Because it was kind of a mixture of something small blossoming into something bigger, successful, but then also I did have some people early on that said it wouldn't work, that I was too young and that I shouldn't have done it. It was interesting, I even had college students who actually joined the church when we started but part of them being college students running their mouths before they were like he's a good preacher and teacher and does Bible study but he's too young, he should be working with somebody else instead of starting his own church. And then some of them actually came and joined as members while they were at school, some stayed, it was for me it's been kind of a mixture so I would say other.

Participant E	The signs for me once again, back to the third question the sign for me when I see that person's lives are being changed, people testifying of how the ministry I provided impacted them, changed their lives, changed their family's lives it provokes me, encourages me to do more.
Participant F	I would think it would be provoking to servanthood. I think that the Lord empowered me to minister because I was a servant. Because I was a servant I think that's how God did it. It was a God thing, it wasn't anything I'd done, I was just as happy being on the piano, playing being over the choir, happy in that realm. It wasn't something I craved or desired. I believe it was always on my life. God had shown me a vision years before that I would pastor and the church would be red. I never even realized it because at the time I went to be associate pastor we didn't even have red pews, we had brown chairs. So the Lord showed me years later that that's what he was calling me to do.
Participant G	I guess this is another other. I think that for me it is to understand where God is moving, where he is calling me to and then finding myself there. That guarantees me number one that I am in the will of God. And if you are in the will of God you cannot fail. You may experience failure here and there but ultimately you will see the kind of success so knowing that God was calling for this or calling me there, to do this or that, it brought a motivation to pour my all into it because I knew the ultimate outcome would be successful. It would cause to the other points you raised or options that were there when some may have said when it could not be done, I understood what God was saying or resilient in the process and also seeing something well really you start with nothing and it becomes something. But at the base of it all the foundation is the fact we are where God is. Many times pastors if they are not careful they will go somewhere, do something, start something, and then ask God to come along and bless it. As opposed to finding where God is moving what he is saying and doing. And to get with that we try to get God to come along with our program.

Question 7: What infrastructures did you put in place to help you stay the task in ministry both naturally and spiritually?	
Participant A	The ministry needed structure, a path that kept me grounded and close to God both naturally and spiritually. Prayer services were important. With my training, I found Bible study, Sunday school, and other academic classes relevant to the success of the ministry. As a musical person, I love anointed music ministry. Mentoring is important. I searched out and found other successful leaders and used their stories and experience to build upon.

| Participant B | I was a Sunday school buff. I loved Sunday school. One of the mothers of that time gave me a book. I think the name of it was Holbert Story of the Bible, it was something like that. In that book was information that was not in the Bible. So I had answers to questions that other young people in my age group didn't have. So Sunday school for me it was exciting because I could ask those questions nobody had the answer but me. I enjoyed Sunday school, that was something I really enjoyed and that intensified my wanting to learn more and develop more. The Sunday school part of it at that time we had YPWW, which was Young People Willing Workers, and we were involved in that heavily. We had a great small group of young people who met every week for Bible study, for prayer or fellowship engagement. One of the mothers of our church had us over every week. Every week we would go over to her house for prayer, Bible study, fun and games and eat. That relationship in fact, most of those young people are still in church today. The kind of relationship that we had going on back then that kept us in church kept us grounded and helped to solidify our relationship with Christ. It was just a great time back then. We are missing that now that we don't have the opportunity to do that kind of fellowship and have those kinds of relationships on an on-going basis. It was something that solidified us, kept us all in church, kept us strong we did a lot of praying, a lot of things of that sort, to keep us strong trying to keep this flesh under subjection as young people and those were the things that kept us going. There was a young friend of mine, his name was Walt Williams. We were just young people trying to do something for God and we developed a ministry for young people. We had a citywide youth choir. Every Friday night we would take our young people to a pizza place, buy all the pizza, bought potato chips, we laughed, talked and the name of that program was Off the Street. It was designed to get young people off the streets on Friday nights to bring them together to fellowship. We did a thing where we all dressed up in tuxedos, we all went out to a luxurious place and had dinner with our little girlfriends. Those were the kinds of things we did to keep all of us solidified and keep us in the church. We kept something going on. We were not bored at all. |
| Participant C | Again, I'm going to say all of those because the Sunday school, Bible studies, it helped me to get where I am. And again music, lot of people don't realize and understand music, that sets the tone for the service for God to come in and move in like he does with his kind of glory. So, I'm going to say, all of the above in addition to all of those, the infrastructure which is basically the foundation is a genuine and sincere desire to walk close with God. Because so many times we are trying to build without hearing God. How solid can your foundation be if you are not really hearing God? All of the above. |

Participant D	It would probably be the educational ministries. That has probably been one of the bedrocks that we focused on, whether that is Bible study, try to do solid preaching, training classes, youth ministry so yes for us, really it's been trying to anchor things on the Word, trying to help people grow in their understanding of the Word and how to understand and hopefully apply it.
Participant E	I'm just going to say prayer. Prayer has been my foundation. Our ministry has been built on prayer from the time I started I committed to leading the church in prayer at a dedicated time every single week; I prayed with the church. When I first started, I pastored two churches but I prayed with that first church every week. So from then until now, fifteen years I've done this. There's been seasons like now where I pray every day with the church. There have also been seasons that I prayed three times a day with the church. Prayer; it's it.
Participant F	I'll say two things. The Lord gave me through Bishop Chapman three mentors if you will as a young person. One was Drew Sheard, Eric Slack, the other one was Joel Lyles. He told those three people to take care of my son. That was in a leadership conference probably, I was just an associate pastor, it was many years ago. Those three men have kept me grounded. They have kept me, I have been able to sound off to them, I've been able to, and it's good because we all need that. That was good for me. That would be the first part and in the second part, I would think that the music ministry has been very impactful in my life. Very, very impactful. It has paid. I had a member of our church who said, "Pastor, you can pray, sing, and preach." And for different reformations that's big. You know in the Baptist Church, they want you to be able to sing, pray, and preach. So I would think that has been a very impactful foundation in my life.

Participant G	For me I think really organizing the church that I serve in such a way that I could fulfill my assignment, so that means developing a structure that supported the vision, ministry, that supported the vision through various ministries, auxiliaries, there's a very strategic organization, in turn, administration, financial administration, and taking all of those components organizing them and placing people where they perhaps have a calling or their best strength is manifested. Then on the personal side my naturally perspective I guess you can say with spirituality is really managing my time and balancing giving that you know pastoring, family first of all, husband and father, pastor, bishop, working with our national church and just in the community, things that we are doing really putting myself on a time schedule daily as well as in addition to building an infrastructure organizationally, administratively at the local level. There's a group I have I lean on for the jurisdiction. And there's a group I lean on for the national AIM convention. I try not to cross-pollinate if I can say it like that these people are specific to those areas. I have an administrator who handles my personal calendar, I have a church secretary that handles exclusively everything relative for Citadel, so on and so forth. And so just building different infrastructures and I know that requires me to be able to go into those different circles and then put on a different hat just depend on what the circumstances are. I don't know if that answered your question.

Question 8: How does establishing an inner circle of other pastors in your circle of ministry help you?	
Participant A	Having an inner circle of other pastors is important for my relationship with other pastors. A trusted friend or confidant is warranted, having a counterpart to share the burden of ministry, it provides good accountability and I find strength in fellowship.

Participant B	Wow, you know pastors in the position that they're in, working with people on a daily basis takes a lot out of them, it drains them of their energy, emotionally, mentally, physically because they are on call twenty four hours. It's unfortunate that the horizontal relationship that inner circle you just mentioned that people we can go to we can trust, people we can feel safe around, people we know who will give us honest report of ourselves and that's for me is missing. I don't know a lot of pastors who have an inner circle where they can feel safe. Where they can say, "You know, I am dealing with an issue I have a problem, will you pray for me to help me get through this and do it in a level of confidentiality that they can trust." That is very few and far between. For me, you know you get kind of leery because you don't have that kind of person you can talk to and pour out to and that's unfortunate. I don't know if a lot of our pastors have that, I'm sure it would be helpful if we had that kind of ministry going on particular today because of stress, so much strain, trying to do things that we do and sometimes you just need somebody to talk to. As a matter of fact, I was talking to someone, we had a conference call today a Zoom call with the bishops, one of the bishops said, "You know maybe this is just something we need to do on a regular basis, just talk." Just deal with the issues all of us are facing. To understand you are not the only one dealing with this. You are not the only one going through this. You're not the only one trying to figure all this out. You don't feel like you're out there by yourself and no one understands what's going on. So we need that kind of relationship at a much greater level than we see it going on today. It is unfortunate, we can't find that safe place in the church. There are things that some pastors are dealing with. If they would tell somebody things that's really going on the inside, they would be shut out, excommunicated. Being in the position you are in, "How could you be doing that?" We don't have that kind of place where we can go. I know some people take for example; T. D. Jakes, has his I don't know if he still has his mega-conference or not but I know people who have gone to those kinds of conferences just to release themselves and deliver themselves and free themselves from things because whoever they are talking to they will probably never see them again, so they are free to relieve themselves so they are able to get that shame or burden off of them so they can be liberated to be free to do what God wants them to do. Unfortunately, we don't have that. We need that ministry.

Participant C	Again, all of the above. I truly believe that all of us especially as a pastor, we need someone to pour into us. We are always pouring out. I just made an illustration with my children that were all here, if I'm constantly pouring into someone and no one is pouring back into me, I'm empty and before you know it when someone needs something from me I'm empty, because I don't have nothing to give. So when you have that inner circle where you can confide in someone, trust in someone, that really does help and also the reason I said other I was listening to I believe it was T. D. Jakes one time said something that sparked a thought with me. One of the reasons why I like to get with other pastors because they understand what I'm experiencing or going through. In addition to that, it gives me a sense of hearing something different, looking at it from a different perspective and if everyone I hang around is people like me, I would never get stronger in my weak areas. Because they're just like me. They think like I would, they digest everything like I do. So I would never get stronger in the areas I am weak because they are going to mirror everything I say and do. When you have that offset, that balance with someone different they may be stronger in the areas I am weak and help bring something to the table and areas they are weak might be stronger in a particular area and be able to help them so that's the reason I would say the other. I tried not to look at the questions, I wanted it to come from here, my heart.
Participant D	Other, because I think it's all of those for me, it's having those people you can trust, those you can be accountable with, and also people who will understand. God knows it can be lonesome out here, if you don't intentionally develop that circle that's going to help keep you accountable that can be trusted, keep pushing you.
Participant E	I would say having a trusted confidant and sharing the burden of ministry, those both. I could elaborate on that but I believe those answers are really acceptable.
Participant F	I'm going to say the very first one is accountability. I think we have to be accountable to one another. I can call a Pastor Terence Hayes and vent, be able to share. I think we need that because pastoral ministry is unlike any other. Out of all the gifts that are in Ephesians pastoring stands out. I think that accountability would be first and you do need a circle, you can't tell everybody what you're going through, there is a burden of pastoral ministry that only pastors can understand. So I would say the very first one is accountability.
Participant G	I want to say good accountability, that could mean a number of things. Because it speaks of friendship they become a confidant but also a sounding board, that accountability piece. Also, reflects someone that's connected to you being in touch with the feelings of your infirmities. Offer whether its spiritual, prayerful, counseling support throughout the life as my role as a pastor and minister so I value pastoral relationships greatly.

Question 9: What preparations have you made to serve in the role of a senior pastor?	
Participant A	My preparation to serve in the role of a senior pastor came mostly by self-study, mentorship with trusted and respected leaders. Lastly, the support of family has been my greatest encouragement.
Participant B	I have done all those things, especially the educational aspect of it. I kind of I guess it's my thought, years ago when I first entered ministry. An old Baptist minister he said, "Kimbrough, you need to go to school." I'm like at that time I'm like man I am Church of God in Christ, I'm Holy Ghost filled, fire baptized, I don't need to go to school. I told him I can just preach the gospel and let the Holy Ghost do the rest. I don't need school. Little did I know, I needed school. Eventually a little late, but eventually I did go and I did acquire a degree and of course you know I'm working on another one now. But going to school is one thing I did to prepare myself watching and observing other men who are in position of leadership what they are doing and how they were doing it. Doing a lot of investigation as to what other ministries are doing as it relates to ministry, trying to prepare someone to succeed me which makes sure that what whatever point in time you know God says, "OK it's time to come home." There will be somebody in place that can take the ministry on and all the work done prior to myself in the life of the late Bishop Mack E. Jonas and the life of the late Bishop Robert L. Chapman, all of that work won't be in vain. Because I would have provided someone, prepared someone, positioned someone to take over, and keep that ministry going until it's time for them to go off the scene and God sends somebody else.
Participant C	All three of those, educational goals, mentorship, respect for others, all of that I would say would be my answer to that question.

Participant D	Again I would say, other. Because I probably have done all of those. The educational piece, the self-study, mentor thing, I've done it but it's probably been much more over the past ten to twelve years prior to that it was a little different for me because I think I was always trying to find it because I really felt I did not have a spiritual father, per se. I know the pastor that I started preaching under is still the pastor at my home church. Good guy, we were never close and I was never even before when we had a previous pastor, this guy was an evangelist and he would come do revivals. I was never even as a kid highly impressed with his preaching, it wasn't bad, it was just, it didn't resonate with me a lot. So although I respected him as pastor, there was not really a closer relationship so I really for years, before I started, I sounded like Moses being on the backside of the mountain, I was young, little less wise, I would make comments like, "Everything I learned were on the backside of the mountain." I don't need, I remember telling one pastor, when I first moved to North Carolina, I told him I'm just being upfront with you, "I'm not looking for a spiritual father, I never had one, God taught me what I needed to know, I'm here at your church because God told me I needed to be." When I look back at it now I was twenty-four, bold running your mouth, talking to this man, I'm like wow, that was extreme. But over time I kind of recognized and realize that my pastor was not necessarily my spiritual father, that I did have connection with people before that had known me and seen me helped me, so it kind of helped me and open my mind to this whole concept of mentoring, being mentored, and listening and being shaped and molded by the experiences of others. That's my long answer for other.
Participant E	I would say all the above. Education, not just my seminary training, I have a Masters of Divinity, not only that, being mentored by season pastors and other education like leadership development training and pastoral leadership conferences.
Participant F	I'm going to say it would be educational and also mentorship. I have been to a few conferences and what has really blessed me and I haven't been in the last couple of years or so, but Bishop Jakes has a conference that I was able to attend and I still to this day can glean from the notes that I took in those three-day conferences. It was a small one it was the Gideon one, that is held at the beginning of the year and I'm telling you even to this day I will go back in my iPad and I really hunger and thirst for more education its different being bivocational and dealing with our everyday lives, our families and but I do hunger for great knowledge and to be around people that soar in the educational realm.
Participant G	I can say all the above. All of that great mixture. Want to make sure that nothing is left out of that. But I will say all of the above if that could be an option.

Question 10: How did you navigate challenging moments in your ministry?	
Participant A	There is no getting away from challenging moments. I navigated through these moments with a prayer life, hiding the Word of God close to my heart, resilience, and grit to press onward despite the circumstances. To be clear, always knowing within my heart, that I am called by God.
Participant B	There again all of those things as I mentioned earlier, the first pastorate I had, I was young. I'm sure I made a lot of mistakes but after that incident, I felt like a failure, I felt defeated. But I wasn't ready to quit. I knew in my heart in my mind and I knew that God had called me to ministry and because I knew that and I was assured of that I wasn't ready to quit. I inquired of God and prayed that he open up a door in which he did and he manifested himself in a way that was just incredible. My father got saved under my ministry. That was a highlight under my ministry. My brother-in-law got saved under my ministry, Pastor McIntyre. These were men who I looked up to, one was my dad the other my brother-in-law, neither one of them were churchmen. My father came to my revival. I did a two-week revival. The last night my wife invited my father to come and he said, "OK." He came the very last night of that two-week revival and gave his life to Christ. That night and he was my first deacon. A month later, Pastor McIntyre came in, gave his heart to God, he was my second deacon. God moved like that. In the middle of winter, in December, snowing a lot and we had a revival that started off was supposed to be one week ended up being a month and a half. We were packing the place out, snow was on the ground a foot deep, God was moving, people were healed, people were delivered, and it was that kind of manifestation of God's power in my life, in my ministry, that let me know you can make it. Those challenging moments but yet God manifested himself and let me know I'm not gone leave you. I brought you out here to bring you in.

Participant C	All of the above and other. I thank God for a prayer life because I truly don't see how a person can make it without a prayer life. God showed me something one time. I was at work talking to an employee and I asked her to do something for me. She was on the other side of the counter. She said, "I can't hear you." I said, "Well, come here." She started moving closer to me. My pitch wasn't any higher and I repeated myself and as she drew closer to me she heard me clear. That's what prayer life has done for me. As I draw closer to God when things really get rough and tough I have to hear God. I have to. This is not the time for me to start asking God for forgiveness, all this other stuff that sometimes can interfere with the connection, but my prayer life keeps me in tune with God all the time so when those trying times do come God gives me direction, he gives me hope. There is a scripture where he talks about, patience, is experience, experience that gets me through those rough times because he tells me I brought you through that last year, so that gives me experience what I'm going through now, so it gives me that hope, so that would be my answer to that plus the other.
Participant D	It's other. Doing all of those. I mean, yes, prayer life, holding to the Word, what I believe God said in his Word, what I believe God said to me but I have, I look back at it now there was still a high level of resilience, and grit that in the moment I didn't realize quite as much. I think I saw it as this is me pushing through it because of my prayer life, my reliance on what God has said in his written Word and proclaimed Word and didn't. I think over time I come to realize that grit and resilience is key to helping those things stick together. It's not solely grit and resilience because that cuts out God but without it; I've seen many people not make it through challenges that I think they could have and I thought they were people of the Word, people of prayer, so I think my prayer life, locked in the Word, resilience, grit all worked together to get me through my numerous challenging moments.
Participant E	It was all the above, all the above, in addition to having a support system of people outside of my local church and even city that loved me and were there for me through every up and down of ministry. I could not of made it without a support system. A healthy support system, no way.
Participant F	I want to say first of all it was consecration. The first one and the third one are praying and scripture coupled together. I've had some challenging moments. This is my nineteenth year. There was a time we had a great exodus because of other people, because of other situations and all, but the Lord gave us resilience and now we have doubled back and we are thriving. So I would have to say prayer and scripture because you got to have something in you for it to come out. Absolutely being resilient in ministry and knowing that I'm not going to give up.

Participant G	I want to say A and C. I want to add in there seeking wise counsel. I want to go back to the other question that was asked about of having certain individuals that share the burden of ministry with you. There are various challenges an individual can face in ministry and building church, etcetera. Just not being so proudful to say I don't know when I need help and it may be sometimes relative to things that are not so spiritual, it may be administratively, financially, and it could be spiritual it could be dealing with problematic members. Dealing with something you dealing with personally, just depending on the context and situation. Just having someone as well that you can connect with, connect to. In addition, have your personal prayer life and having that resilience and all of that, and the Word of God associated with it.

Question 11: How important is family life for you as a pastor?	
Participant A	Family life is very meaningful having an immediate family to help in ministry. You need someone to provide you with a sense of support and strength. I love modeling the behavior of being a husband, having a wife as a great example from the Word of God.

Participant B	You can't say too much about the family. I am a very fortunate man because when I was coming along they taught us, God, church and everything else comes along after that. All of my time, all of my free time, vacation time, and all that kind of stuff was given to the church. We never went on vacation. We went to Memphis for the National Call meeting, we went to the National Convocation, and we took our kids to all of those events, but a vacation for a family in that respect we didn't know that because we were, I was so committed to the church and its teachings and its doctoral tenets and one day my wife told me she says, "You're losing your sons." I'm like, what are you talking about. She let me know your sons growing up, they don't know who you are because you are never here. That rocked me. The thing that really got me the most was my daughter. She came to me one day and said, "Dad, can I be a member of your church?" I like, "What, you are already a member of my church." She said, "No, I want to be like everybody else. I want to be able to come into your office and talk to you, like all the other members do." Man, that blew me away. I mean I just, I didn't know what to say. It shook me. I had to start prioritizing my family. Give my family time. Before I hadn't done that. I was fortunate that God, because in my ignorance, he blessed me. And allowed my family, my children to love the church, and love God and they are in the ministry now, and you know that and it's because God honored my ignorance and my sacrifice to him. He knew what I was doing to him with a true heart to serve him so he blessed my effort. So my family is together, they are tight, my kids work in the church, they have ministries in the church, and it's just been a blessing to have them in the ministry that I oversee. It's incredible. We have a great family and I tell anybody that strong families make strong churches. If you don't have a strong family you are not going to have a strong church. That's just the way it is. Families are very important, and I tell young men now its God, then your family and you know, church. I told a bishop not long ago, "Jesus died for the church, so I don't have to die for the church." Jesus did that two thousand years ago, I learned that now. Take out more time with my family now than I use to do. Families are important they are the foundational basis in what we do in ministry.

Participant C	I'm going to say all of the above again and other. I think this is the way I feel personally. I have scriptures to support it, it would take an hour. I truly believe if you have family, I truly believe that is our first calling. And if we don't take care of our home according to scripture so I truly believe all of the above and others. When you have family involved, I thought about Myles Munroe, we talked about this before once that success without a successor is failure. Success without a successor is failure. If everything I have and know and I don't share it with my children, my children's children and I go to my grave; how successful really was I? And if I impart, what I know, whatever that is that means to me that is success because it doesn't die if I die. Who better else than to pour into our family because generally speaking they have the same spirit. Sometimes a different building but the same foundation.
Participant D	The second one, having family there for support. That is really key for me. One thing I have always tried to raise up I was the one called to pastor not my family. But I do know that puts burdens on them, but I have tried not to overburden my children or my wife with regards to that. So having them there for support, that is key.
Participant E	It's very important. I am definitely very much committed to my family, very much committed to trying to find the balance time-wise, spending time letting them know they are important, but also I want my family to know God. Ministry for me starts at home.
Participant F	I think it's very meaningful. I've watched my family and I took a tip from Bishop Chapman who didn't do a lot of things with his sons. To the point he always said, "James, make sure your family is close to you." I take it very seriously family life, balance is very important to me. My wife has been with me in ministry. My oldest daughter has done things in the ministry and she is not in church, but she does all our graphics, she's working on our web design and this past summer the Lord has allowed her and my other daughter they did all our women bathrooms, put flooring down, the whole nine. Painted it and so it's a blessing for me because we need our families with us. My wife, when I beg her and push her to preach she will preach for me. I tell her she was called before I was called. She is a woman of God that can proclaim the Word of God. So I think it's very important, it's pivotal, now. I think we have to be careful because we need their support, we need them undergirding us, they're prayers, because they see what everybody else doesn't see. So I think it is critical.

Participant G	What is the importance of the family life for a pastor? To me that's a pastor's first ministry. I could be wrong but I do not believe any individual ought to attempt to pastor, or minister, especially in this context of pastoral ministry. If their family life is not where it needs to be, the Bible speaks of how can one manage, rule the house of God, and not able to manage the affairs of his own home. The qualifications of a bishop and a deacon are one that rules his own house well, and that his children, family reflects of the ministry he or she has projected. And so family life really is the foundation. It is important, and I know I'm not speaking in terms of some of the options that were there regardless of whether they are involved in terms of helping. Now it is a blessing to have their support, help, and involvement. You want that too. I think that will happen but foundationally I think that the first ministry is home, the wife, the children, ensuring you are the priest, the prophet, the provider of your home. If you are unsuccessful of being the priest, provider, protector of your home, then how are you going to do that as a pastor? A pastor is a priest, prophet, protector and provider of a local congregation. I say that is the primary first ministry of any pastor.

Question 12: How necessary are finances to establishing ministry?	
Participant A	Ministry requires finances to survive. It is vital and important to expand the work of ministries. I follow as close as I can to Matthew 6:33, "But seek ye first the kingdom of God and his righteousness; and all these things shall be added unto you."

Participant B	Since money is the medium of exchange on this planet, if you don't have any money you are not going to get very far, you are not going to do a whole lot as it relates to ministry. Ministry cost. We always say salvation is free and that's true but to do ministry it's going to cost you because there are so many things involved that especially in today's culture perhaps years ago they didn't worry about. Pastor was the pastor of the church, maybe his daughter was the secretary, maybe his son was the drummer and maybe his wife was something else, but today that is not the case. We have a staff, we have to worry about the secretary, we have custodians, got musicians, maintenance on buildings, the repair and upkeep and all these things, all that stuff cost money. Jesus in the Word of God spoke more about money more than he did anything else. It's unfortunate that for us money is almost a bad word. If you start talking about money in our church people start getting fidgety, nervous, and wonder, what are you doing with all that money? We trying to keep the church going is what we are trying to do. It just takes a lot of money to reach out, reach souls, support other missions on the other side of the world and particularly in our church we are involved with 102 churches in the world so you know sometimes we try to send something to support those ministries so all of that costs. Money is absolutely necessary if you are going to have an effective ongoing ministry. You can't get around it.
Participant C	I'm going to say all the above and other. Definitely, all of above because I've learned personally that you can be anointed, have friends, you need money to pay bills. You really do. For me when you get a plan and work it you get a little money on the side or savings it really feels good, takes a lot of pressure off you. Nothing worse than in ministry as a leader to have too much pressure on you. When you don't have money to pay bills, when you don't have money to see things, that's a lot pressure. And another area that I'm learning our members man I don't care what size building you have, they want to see a progressive church. Every now and then, buy a new lamp. A floor mat, something. If you don't have any money you can't make that happen, so the people get disgruntled. Before you know it they're talking about leaving, what you're doing with my money so, on and so on.
Participant D	Vital and the second one expanding it is true you have to have finances to do ministry. But I don't ever I don't ever try not to ever put finances above God, because I know God can provide but I do acknowledge the fact having finances does help you expand some things, increase what you're offering, the reach of what you're doing. That is vitally important; we have to be careful not to raise money higher than God. Because God will provide rather that's stretching, whether that's sending somebody to give however it works, but I think even though we are trusting God to provide we can't get somewhere and think finances are not important and not doing something with them.

Participant E	I think all of the above. It's very important. You cannot execute without the capacity to do certain things. Finance is important to fund the vision. The finances being in order meticulously will make your ministry attractive for more funding to do what you need to do. And the call of God on our lives needs to be financed.
Participant F	It's vital for kingdom work. It's very essential, we can't do ministry without money. The finances, the Lord has to give us wisdom of how we are to execute. Have you retired yet? So you understand bivocational of how we have poured out of our funds into the ministry for it to be instrumental and for other people to rally around us; this beautiful edifice that you all have to pour in resources, so it's very important, it's for kingdom, it's for the ministry to be expanding, for exposure, for you to be able to bring people in that can assist you and help you in ministry so I think it's vital.
Participant G	If I can answer it like this, I know I just jacked up your whole survey of research process. I'm not sure who came up with this but I subscribe to it. "People plus money equal ministry." The context I believe of that and suggest that in this world there is a matter of exchange and resources of finances are critical to operating and conducting ministry and it goes back to what I was saying earlier about family dynamics, the idea of finances and money are so critical for a leader, number one he must have integrity, and know how to manage and manage well in terms of the financial perspective and it is very necessary that funds and monies are available to enhance and move forward the work of God. What is critical is especially when you're starting out you have limited resources and the significance is you be found faithful at managing what you have until God blesses you with more. Manage it well, just because you don't have what the next pastor has down the street doesn't mean that what you have is not as significant it's just the season and process and the level you are in an understand you cannot further the work of God without the financial support and so I guess to piggyback on some of the options that are there it is instrumental to do great exploits, it's not the only thing that is needed but it is instrumental and it's important to expand the work of God. The Bible says and the Lord gave to every one of those servants according to their several abilities. Which means their capacity to be able to manage at that level. I will say this and stop. There was a superintendent here in Memphis who said this all the time, "You can tell more about a man of how he manages his money than you can by how he shouts and dance, preach, and speaks in tongues." Money speaks and says a lot. Jesus said, wherever your heart is there will be your treasure also. I think is very significant that financial support means and management and be part of the pastor's leadership in ministry.

Results

Theme Development

The thematic analysis of this research captured a consistent pattern of four themes that reflected a common narrative of the lived experiences of the senior pastors. Robert Yin states, "The studies strive to be as faithful as possible to the lived experiences, especially as might be described by the participants' own words" (2011, 15). The lived experiences of each of these men were the determining factors that contributed to their long-term tenure as servants of God in ministry.

Table 5 presents the themes identified as prevalent elements from an examination of the participants' combined responses:

**Table 5. Prevailing themes from research participants'
combined responses**

Item	Theme
1	Prayer
2	Servanthood
3	Success
4	Making a Difference

Prayer

Prayer is a common theme that radiated in the conversation with the pastors participating in this phenomenological research study. Prayer is a strong spiritual discipline that is the foundation of Church of God in Christ, and it is practiced and encouraged with all the men and women who are part of this great church. In a textbook for ordination with this church, there is a passage that reads, "Our founder, Bishop Mason was known nationwide for his ardent spiritual disciplines, including extended fasting, protracted daily praying, and dedication (Johnson, Hall, Daniels, and Herndon 2019, 311).

Prayer catapults us into the frontier of the spiritual life. Of all the spiritual disciplines, prayer is the most central because it ushers us into perpetual communion with the Father (Johnson, Hall, Daniels, and Herndon 2019, 310).

Along with prayer comes consecration. "The history of COGIC is replete with great saints who exercised great spiritual discipline and demonstrated models of spiritual formation that we can draw upon today" (Johnson, Hall, Daniels, and Herndon 2019, 311).

Table 6 presents participant responses supporting the identification of prayer as a prevalent theme.

Table 6. Participant responses supporting the identification of prayer as a prevalent theme

1. Prayer Theme	
Participant A	The ministry needed structure, a path that kept me grounded and close to God both naturally and spiritually. Prayer services were important.
Participant B	It was something that solidified us, kept us all in the church as young people coming along in ministry. We did a lot of praying, a lot of things of that sort, to keep us strong trying to keep this flesh under subjection.
Participant C	I thank God for a prayer life because I truly don't see how a person can make it without a prayer life. As I draw closer to God when things get rough and tough I have to hear God, I have to.

Participant D	I had a prayer life, holding on the Word, what I believe God said in his Word, what I believe God said to me but I have to look back now that there was still a high level of resilience, and grit at the moment I didn't realize quite as much. I think I saw it as this is me pushing through it because of my prayer life, my reliance on what God has said in his written Word, and proclaimed Word and didn't think over time to come to realize that grit and resilience are key to help those things stick together.
Participant E	Prayer has been my foundation. It has been, our ministry has been built on prayer from the time I started I committed to leading the church in prayer at a dedicated time every single week; I prayed with the church. When I first started, I pastored two churches but I prayed with the first church every week. So from then until now, fifteen years I've done this. There have been seasons like now where I pray every day with the church. There have also been seasons that I prayed three times a day with the church.
Participant F	I want to say first of all it was consecration. Having prayer and the scripture is important because you have to have something in you for it to come out. ... Being resilient in ministry and knowing that I'm not going to give up.

Success in Ministry

Success can be measured by others as it pertains to ministry in a quantifiable way. How many members do you have? The pastors in this research had various demographics, with their various membership sizes ranging from small to large. A small church average attendance is fifty or fewer people, medium average attendance is fifty-one to three hundred people, and large average attendance is between 301 and two thousand people (www.usachurches.org). The interest of this research was driven to acknowledge there are successful pastors serving in the Church of God in Christ that are both small and large, with them both being successful at the same time.

Linwood authored a book titled *Engineering Your Vision: Seven*

Principles for Obtaining Ultimate Success in Every Area of Your Life. A passage from the book reads, "If you desire success in every aspect of your life, learn to have faith. Once you have it exercise it!" (2015, 117).

Table 7 presents participant responses supporting the identification of success in ministry as a prevalent theme.

Table 7. Participant responses supporting the identification of success in ministry as a prevalent theme

2. Success in Ministry Theme	
Participant B	Professional development and spiritual growth are absolutely for success in ministry. You cannot be stagnant, you have to work at being all you can be and being the best you can be as it relates to leadership and that is an everyday ongoing process you are working constantly to improve who you are as a man or woman of God. ... Being successful is fulfilling the assignment you have been given by God. When you fulfill that assignment then you are successful because it's only at that point that God can say, "Well done, good and faithful servant."
Participant D	I see success as fulfilling what God has called you to do and what that might look like is different based upon who you are and where you are, and what you are called to do. ... I don't only see ministry success is not only individualistic or in the sense of solely about numbers, but also what type of impact are you having that may not necessarily be quantifiable, in the traditional aspect of doc, how many are you running, what you looking at, that type of thing.
Participant E	I define success as impacting lives. I think when you have a vision you execute that vision to completion and when it has impacted one or more lives I believe that is success. To me, success is completing your assignment. Whatever that is and so, that's how I measure it. I've learned that whatever it is that God has assigned to your hand and whoever it is he has put in your path to influence; when you do that, you are successful.

| Participant G | For me, success in ministry reflects a ministry that is fulfilling the purpose of the assignment and the call of the ministry that God has given them. I believe there is a unique call that God may have for us and we find ourselves pursuing that vision and pursing that mission and when we do that. To me, that's the definition of success. |

Servanthood

Servanthood. The pastors shared a common attitude of how they see the work they do on a daily basis that captured my attention. In serving God, there comes a time when prioritizing the task at hand matters; it matters most to God. "Therefore, glorify God in your body and in your spirit" (1 Corinthians 6:20 KJV). The author Kevin Bond writes, "The servant who is unwilling to surrender to God is not a servant of God, but of himself. Either we serve God or we're serving ourselves" (2007, 99).

In the Church of God in Christ, senior pastors are honored in a certain way for the service and support they render to the members in their congregations. Many pastors are rewarded for the commitment, dedication, and time they give to the families in their times of sorrow, marriages, baby christenings, and many more ministerial duties. One of the most common things you will see is a pastor's anniversary. This anniversary is for the years of ministry served. The most common biblical theme you see in a pastor's congregation is "Let the elders who rule well be counted worthy of double honor" (1 Timothy 5:17 KJV). These men are not only honored, but the focus is the fact they have served. "And whoever will be chief among you, let him be your servant" (Matthew 20:27 KJV).

A servant is someone who is able to lead as well as follow, one who is bold, confident, and dependable (Bond 2007, 106).

Table 8 presents participant responses supporting the identification of servanthood as a prevalent theme.

Table 8. Participant responses supporting the identification of servanthood as a prevalent theme

3. Servanthood Theme	
Participant A	It was further important for me to make a difference in God's kingdom working and serving with a servant's heart. … Always knowing within my heart, that I am called by God."
Participant B	I was fortunate that God, because in my ignorance, he blessed me. And allowed my family, my children love the church and in my ignorance and my sacrifice to him. He knew that what I was doing to him with a true heart to serve him so he blessed my effort.
Participant E	I began ministry when I was a toddler and I think as I began to grow, becoming older I began to connect my life experiences with the call to assist people, also had experienced some of the things that I and my family did. I felt my purpose on earth.
Participant F	I want to make a difference in Christendom with a servant's heart. My story is I succeeded a great man. An heir, it propelled me into pastorship. … I would think it would be provoking to servanthood. I think the Lord empowered me to minister because I was a servant. Because I was a servant that's how God did it. It was a God thing. It wasn't anything, I was just as happy being on the piano, playing and being over the choir, happy in that realm.
Participant G	Having a heart of servanthood is very significant in understanding the role of a senior pastor. As we all understand Jesus said, "Whoever is greatest among you be the servant of all." Accepting that role and responsibility as a pastor most definitely there must have been a heart matter.

Making a Difference

"The true servant leader must not be selfish, but generous towards those whom he serves. Whether through the impartation of knowledge and advice, or the offering of some other assistance, he must willingly share that which God has given them to build the kingdom, without holding information that can benefit others" (Bond 2007, 84).

Senior pastors share their lives with many people. It takes a balanced leader to extend time to their own families as well as the people they serve on a weekly basis. It makes a huge statement when one can be selfless. "Constantly pursing your own needs, wants, and desires creates a toxic culture. Leaders must not focus on what only benefits them, but what is most beneficial to the project and its builders" (Davis 2015, 115).

The years invested in a ministry should see one for sure thing: a person's life greatly changed from where they began in their life. Senior pastors have the grave task and responsibility to feed the flock they have been entrusted to serve. It is through strong, kind, empathetic, yielding, and humble leadership that a leader understands everything they offer to the people of God is to help make a difference in the day-to-day lives, making true disciples for Christ.

Table 9 presents participant responses supporting the identification of making a difference as a prevalent theme.

Table 9. Participant responses supporting the identification of making a difference as a prevalent theme

4. Making a Difference Theme	
Participant A	It was further important for me to make a difference in God's kingdom working and serving with a servant's heart. Making disciples of men was the biggest factor.

Participant C	I genuinely want to make a difference in someone's life. When you can take what God has given you and help others with it, that just drives me. It just absolutely drives me. That passion to make a difference in someone's life for me there is nothing more rewarding when you hear someone say, "You were responsible for saving my life." And for me, that is like water on a seed. When I hear, "Listen, you made a difference in my life," that in itself produces life in me.
Participant D	For me it was making a difference in Christendom. I felt God calling.
Participant E	When I see that person's lives are being changed, people testifying of how the ministry I provided impacted them, changed their lives, changed their family's lives it provokes me, encourages me to do more.
Participant F	I want to say making a difference in Christendom with a servant's heart.

Research Questions

1. What is it about a ministry that gave some pastors the resilience and tenacity to become a long-tenured pastor?
2. What gave some pastors the strength and ability to work through difficulties that earned them the title of senior pastor?
3. What are the innate talents or abilities possessed by some pastors and implemented in their ministry that enabled a long-term tenure?

The pastors provided insightful and resourceful answers to the research questions posed for this research. A pastor is styled as a shepherd, one who feeds the flock of God. "Therefore, I exhort the elders among you, as your fellow elder and witness of the suffering of Christ, and a partaker also of the glory that is to be revealed. Shepherd the flock of God among you, exercising oversight, not under compulsion, but voluntarily, according to the will of God; and not for sordid gain, but with eagerness: nor yet as lording it over those allotted to your charge, but proving to be examples to the flock" (1 Peter 5:1–4 NASB). The lived experiences of these pastors helped identify what it takes to become a long-term tenured pastor. The three research questions come from a phenomenological research method. "A phenomenological question explores what is given in moments of prereflective, predicative experience-experiences as we live through them" (Manen 2014, 27).

It is important to note with this research question, "Ministry demands resilience! It is next to impossible to function as a servant without it" (Bond 2007, 74).

The effective ministry leader must be able! He must be able to lead, able to take responsibility, able to change, and able to accept changes (Bond 2007, 14). Much like a beautiful field of green grass, ministry is very attractive from afar. When looking across a field, one only sees what appear to be perfectly formed blades of grass, seemingly void of imperfection (Bond 2007, 14). Pastors need the strength and ability to work through difficult moments as senior pastors. The pastors shared how they navigated the waters of difficulty.

Senior pastors take upon the burden of ministry standing and holding onto the Word of God. They possess innate talents or abilities that they use in line with the ministries they serve. "Like the eagle, a servant must be willing to take a stand even if it's a lonely one. He must be willing to soar above all others to get the best possible perspective on every situation. He must never fluctuate in the choices he makes or the path he takes" (Bond 2007, 77–78).

A Calling

In the research, all of the pastors shared how they got into the work of ministry with one key element: the call. When a pastor has the burning passion and desire to enter into this vocation, it has to be solely a God moment. "God appoints certain individuals to serve him in specific vocations of service" (Wilson and Hoffman 2007, 70.) The responses from the research have led me to see how they have reached this plateau of ministry.

One participant displayed unyielding resilience and tenacity that led him to become a long-tenured pastor. A prayer life, resilience, grit to press onward despite the circumstance, and hiding the Word of God close to the heart. He further shared, "There have been seasons like now where I pray every day with the church. There have also been seasons that I prayed three times a day with the church" (interview with participant E, 2020). One of the spiritual disciplines of the Church of God in Christ is prayer. Prayer is powerful; it's a weapon that one must keep locked and loaded to win the battles and challenges encountered in ministry.

A senior participant with years of seniority stated, "There is no getting away from challenging moments. I navigated through these moments with solid spiritual disciplines, prayer, the Word of God, despite the circumstances." Mainly, he said, "To be clear, always knowing within my heart, that I am called by God" (interview with participant A, 2020). One must know without any question they have been called by God to take on this role. "Calling into the ministry is filled with challenges that can easily derail those with less than genuine callings" (Wilson and Hoffman 2007, 66)

A noteworthy moment was when one of the participants experienced a moment that could have made him or break him. He experienced a moment that could have been the deciding factor for whether he continued on in ministry or failed. During his pastorate, one of the churches he served fired him. "I felt like a failure. I felt defeated. But I wasn't ready to quit. I knew in my heart and in my mind that God had called me to ministry, and because I knew that and I was assured that I wasn't ready to quit. I inquired of God and prayed that he opens up a door in which he did, and he manifested himself in a way that was just incredible" (interview with participant B, 2020). This is resilience at its finest!

A Prayer Life

If one had to sum up an ingredient that made the decision to remain in ministry, it has to be the power of prayer. Prayer is a strong presence in the Church of God in Christ. This particular participant made it clear the very thing that sustained him and kept him focused on the work of ministry was a solid prayer life.

> As I draw closer to God when things get rough and tough I have to hear God. This is not the time for me to start asking God for forgiveness, all this other stuff that sometime can interfere with the connection, but my prayer life keeps me in tune with God all the time, so when those trying times do come, God gives me direction. He gives me hope. There is a scripture where he talks about, patience, experiences, the experience that gets me through those rough times because he tells me I brought you through that last year, so that gives me to experience what I'm going through now, so it gives me that hope. (interview with participant C, 2020)

The rich and wise words of Solomon describe hope like this: "Hope deferred makes the heart sick, but a dream fulfilled is a tree of life" (Proverbs 13:12 NLT).

There will be tests, trials, and challenges that come with the work of ministry for pastors. "Our calling must be evaluated and tested to ensure its authenticity" (Wilson and Hoffman 2007, 66). A participant shared how he navigated the challenging moments. "I embraced a prayer life, holding the Word, what I believed God said in his Word, what I believed God said to me." He further stated, "As I look back over it now, there was still a high level of resilience, grit, that at the moment I didn't realize quite as much. It's not solely grit and resilience because that cuts out God but without it; I've seen many people not make it through challenges that I think they could have and I thought they were people of the Word, people of prayer, so I think, yeah, so once again, prayer life, locked into the Word, grit and resilience have all worked together during my numerous challenging moments" (interview with participant D, 2020).

One of the participants expressed a prayer life, resilience, grit, and keeping the Word of God close as the cause of resilience and tenacity in ministry, but he added seeking wise counsel.

> There are various challenges an individual can face in ministry and building a church, etcetera. Just not being so proud to say, 'I don't know,' when I need help and it may be sometime relative to things that are not so spiritual, it may be administratively, financially, and it could be spiritual, it could be dealing with problematic members. Dealing with something you dealing with personally, just depending on the context and situation. Just having someone as well that you can connect with, connect to. Also, have your personal prayer life and having that resilience and all of that, and the word of God associated with it. (interview with participant G, 2020)

One participant shared this: "I'm just going to say prayer. Prayer has been my foundation. It has been, our ministry has been built on prayer from the time I started. I committed to leading the church in prayer at a dedicated time every single week; I prayed with the church. When I first started, I pastored two churches but I prayed with that first church every week. So from then until now, fifteen years I've done this." His passion for education has also been instrumental for him in ministry. "Not just my seminary training. I have a masters of divinity, not only that, mentored by seasons pastors and other education like leadership and development training and pastoral leadership conferences" (interview with participant E, 2020).

Prayer is the mantra for this participant.

> I thank God for a prayer life because I truly don't see how a person can make it without a prayer life. God showed me something one time. I was at work talking to an employee, and I asked her to do something for me. She was on the other side of the counter. She said, "I can't hear you." I said, "Well, come here." She started moving closer to me. My pitch wasn't any higher, and I repeated myself, and as she drew closer to me, she heard me. That's what prayer life has done for me. As I draw closer to God when things get rough and tough I have to hear God. I have to. This is not the time for me to start asking God for forgiveness, all this other stuff that sometimes can interfere with the connection, but my prayer life keeps me in tune with God all the time so when those trying times do come God gives me direction, he gives me hope. There is a scripture where he talks about, patience, experiences, the experience that gets me through those rough times because he tells me I brought you through that last year, so that gives me to experience what I'm going through now, so it gives me that hope, so that would be my answer to that plus other. (interview with participant C, 2020)

This particular participant was transparent about the loss of members in his congregation. "There was a time we had a great exodus because of other people, because of other situations and all, but the Lord gave us resilience, and now we have doubled back, and we are thriving. Being resilient in ministry and knowing that I'm not going to give up" (interview with participant F, 2020). It is clear to me these men were assured of the call to ministry. "One does not choose the ministry! A pastor is chosen" (Wilson and Hoffman 2007, 71).

Strength to Endure

A younger participant in ministry said the things that carried him through trials and moments of difficulty were prayer, resilience, grit to press onward despite the circumstances, and hiding the Word of God in his heart. "Additionally a support system of people outside of my local church and even in the city that loved me and was there for me through every up and down in ministry. I could not have made it without a support system. A healthy support system, no way" (interview with participant E, 2020).

Participant A is the statesman of the senior pastors based on his longevity. "There is no getting away from challenging moments. I navigated through these moments with a prayer life, hiding the Word of God close to my heart, resilience, and grit to press onward despite the circumstances" (interview with Participant A, 2020). One of the powerful revelations of the sustaining power and strength that kept this pastor standing was his acknowledgment of a consecrated and dedicated lifestyle to God. In the ordination process, pastors are consecrated by the laying on of hands by their respective jurisdictional bishops. When these men are consecrated and dedicated to God, it's the strength of God that rests in their hearts. "It was important for me solely because of its obedience to the will of God by living a consecrated life" (interview with participant A, 2020).

A steady temperament is evident in how another participant handles difficulty and circumstances that are challenging to senior pastors. Like many of the pastors, a consistent theme of prayer, resilience, grit, and keeping the Word of God close to the heart was necessary. He further stated,

> I want to add in there seeking wise counsel. I want to be able to go back to the other question that was asked about having certain individuals that share the burden of ministry with you. There are various challenges an individual can face in ministry and building a church, etcetera. Just not being so proud to say I don't know when I need help and it may be sometimes relative to things that are not so spiritual, it may be administratively, financially, and it could be spiritual, it could be dealing with problematic members. Dealing with something you dealing with personally, just depending on the context and situation. Just having someone as well that you can connect with, connect to. Also, have our personal prayer life and having that resilience and all of that, and the word of God associated with it. (interview with participant G, 2020)

Consecration

Of the seven men who shared, two of them mentioned a life of consecration. "I want to say first of all it was consecration. Praying, hiding the word of God in your heart are both coupled together. I've had some challenging moments. This is my nineteenth year" (interview with participant F, 2020). The fact this participant has reached nineteen years of ministry speaks volumes to what has kept him on the path of endurance. It is the spiritual disciplines of the Church of God in Christ that are life changing. Fasting is one of those spiritual disciplines that accompanies a consecrated life. "The spiritual disciplines open the door to a spiritual relationship and fellowship with God. The needed change within us is God's work, not ours" (Johnson, Hall, Daniels, and Herndon 2019, 310).

Pastoring can be a lonely vocation. It was pleasing to learn the importance of mentorship and the assistance pastors need in the Church of God in Christ to endure moments of hardship. One of the participants opened up about his experience with a pastor he was called to serve. "I was young, little less wise, I would make comments like,

> Everything I learned was on the backside of the mountain, I don't need you, "I'm not looking for a spiritual father, I never had one, God taught me what I need to know. I'm here at your church because God told me I needed to be." But over time I recognized and realized that though my pastor was not necessarily my spiritual father, that I did have a connection with people before that, who had known me and seen me, helped me so it kind of helped me and open my mind to this whole concept of mentoring, being mentored, and listening and being shaped and molded by the experiences of others. (interview with participant D, 2020)

"A humble understanding of ourselves is necessary to have a right view of our calling as ministers. Such understanding will prevent us from performing for the crowd and instead encourage us to play to an audience of One" (Wilson and Hoffman 2007, 20).

No greater challenge can bring you to reality than being taken down from a ministerial position. It was no moral failure; it was just the people who chose not to follow this leader. He said it took an experience of failure to face the challenges he encountered in ministry head-on.

The first pastorate I had, I was young. I'm sure I made a lot of mistakes, but after that incident, I felt like a failure, I felt defeated. But I wasn't ready to quit. I knew in my heart, in my mind, and I knew that God had called me to ministry, and because I knew that, I was assured that I wasn't ready to quit. I inquired of God and prayed that he open up a door in which he did and he manifested himself in a way that was just incredible. My father got saved under my ministry. That was a highlight under my ministry. My brother-in-law got saved under my ministry, (name concealed). These were men who I looked up to, one was my dad and the other my brother-in-law neither one of them were churchmen. My father came to my revival. I did a two-week revival. The last night my wife invited my father to come and he said, "OK." He came the very last night of that two-week revival and gave his life to Christ that night and he was my first deacon. A month later, (name concealed) came in, gave his heart to God, he was my second deacon. God moved like that. In the middle of winter, in December, snowing a lot and we had a revival that started was supposed to be one week ended up being a month and a half. We were packing the place out, snow was on the ground a foot deep, God was moving, people were healed, people were delivered, and it was that kind of manifestation of God's power in my life, in my ministry, that let me know you can make it. Those challenging moments but yet God manifested himself and let me know I'm not gone leave you. I brought you out here to bring you in. (interview with participant B, 2020)

Skill Set and Abilities

Senior pastors take upon the burden of ministry, standing and holding onto the Word of God. They possess innate talents or abilities that they use in line with the ministries they serve. "Like the eagle, a servant must be willing to take a stand even if it's a lonely one. He must be willing to soar above all others to get the best possible perspective on every situation. He must never fluctuate in the choices he makes or the path he takes" (Bond 2007, 77–78).

Another participant has coupled his high school education with his military experiences in his ministry. "My preparation to serve in the role of a senior pastor came mostly by self-study, mentorship with trusted and respected leaders. Lastly, the support of family has been my greatest encouragement" (interview with participant A, 2020).

An up-and-coming trend-setting leader among the group has an arsenal of abilities and organizational skills he uses in ministry as a senior pastor.

> For me, I think organizing the church that I serve in such a way that I could fulfill my assignment. That means developing a structure that supports the vision, ministry, through its various ministries, auxiliaries. There's a very strategic organization, in terms of the administration, financial administration, and taking all of those components organizing them and placing people where they perhaps have a calling or their best strength manifested. On the personal side, my natural perspective I guess you can say with spirituality is managing my time and balancing giving that you know pastoring, family first of all, husband and father, pastor, bishop, working with our national church and just in the community, things that we are doing putting myself on a schedule daily as well as in addition to building

a jurisdiction. And there's a group I lean on for the national Auxiliary in Ministry convention (AIM). I try not to cross-pollinate if I can say it like that these people are specific to those areas. I have an administrator who handles my calendar, I have a secretary that handles exclusively everything for Citadel, so on and so forth. And so just building different infrastructures and I know that requires me to be able to go into those different circles and then put on a different hat just depend on what the circumstances are. (interview with participant G, 2020)

This energetic participant added his input on his abilities and talents that have kept him as a long-tenured pastor.

I'll say two things. The Lord gave me through Bishop Chapman three mentors if you will as a young person. One was Drew Sheard, Eric Slack, the other one was Joel Lyles. He told those three people to take care of my son. That was in a leadership conference probably, I was just an associate pastor, it was many years ago. Those three men have kept me grounded. They have kept me, I have been able to sound off to them, I've been able to, and it's good because we all need that. That was good for me. That would be the first part and in the second part, I would think that the music ministry has been very impactful in my life. Very impactful; it has paid. I had a member of our church who said, "Pastor, you can sing and preach, and for different reformations that's big!" You know in the Baptist church they want you to be able to sing pray and preach. So I would think that has been a very impactful foundation in my life. (interview with participant F, 2020)

This participant has a PhD in divinity. This has been an exceptional blessing for him in ministry. "It would probably be the educational ministries. That has been one of the bedrocks that we focused on, whether that is Bible study, try to do solid preaching, training classes, youth ministry so yes for us, really it's been trying to anchor things on the word, trying to help people grow in their understanding of the Word and how to understand and hopefully apply it" (interview with participant D, 2020).

They are the foundational tools one needs to embrace to be relevant in ministry. This participant stated,

> Again, I'm going to say all of those because the Sunday school, Bible studies, it helped me to get where I am. And again music, a lot of people don't realize and understand music, which sets the tone for the service for God to come in and move in as he does with his kind of glory. So, I'm going to say, all of the above in addition to all of those, the infrastructure which is the foundation is a genuine and sincere desire to walk close with God. Because so many times we are trying to build without hearing God. (interview with participant C, 2020)

A participant shared,

> I have done all those things, especially the educational aspect of it. I kind of I guess it's my thought, years ago when I first entered the ministry. An old Baptist, not an old Baptist minister he said, "Kimbrough, you need to go to school." I'm like at that time I'm like, "Man. I am Church of God in

Christ, I'm Holy Ghost filled, fire baptized, I don't need to go to school. I told him I can just preach the gospel and let the Holy Ghost do the rest. I don't need school." Little did I know, I needed school. Eventually a little late, but eventually I did go and I acquired a degree and of course you know I'm working on another one now. But going to school is one thing. I did prepare myself by watching and observing other men who are in a position of leadership what they are doing and how they were doing it. Doing a lot of investigation as to what other ministries are doing as it relates to ministry, trying to prepare someone to succeed me which makes sure that whatever point in time you know God says, "OK it's time to come home," there will be somebody in place that can take the ministry on of all the work done before myself in the life of the late Bishop Mack E. Jonas and the life of the late Bishop Robert L. Chapman, all of that work won't be in vain. Because I would have provided someone, prepared someone, positioned someone to take over, and keep that ministry going until it's time for them to go off the scene and God sends somebody else. (interview with participant B, 2020)

Summary

The lived experiences of the senior pastors serving in the Church of God in Christ revealed the strength, resilience, and tenacity to overcome the obstacles, hardships, and difficulties with a fulfilling and rewarding outcome to succeed as pastors serving their flocks. It was during the interviewing process that I listened with an unbiased attitude and nonjudgment. I listened attentively to the heart of men who are serving in roles as I am. It is even more critical for clergymen to establish trusted, safe, and intimate relationships with other pastors to assure them all pastors experience and encounter similar circumstances. In their vocations as shepherds, each of them carried a common theme of prayer, servanthood, and being successful. Their understanding and sensitivity to the call of God have provided the assurance and clarity for them to walk adeptly in the duty of leading and guiding the souls of men and women in their everyday lives, with spiritual guidance for their well-being. Longevity is a commendable action for today's leaders. "For many are called, but few are chosen" (Matthew 22:14 NASB).

5

CONCLUSION

Overview

The content of this manuscript is research investigating the resilience and success of pastors in the Church of God in Christ, a Pentecostal denomination that has more than six million members, including more than three thousand pastors. The research was a phenomenological study designed to provide a narrative interview of the participants to share their background, role, and day-to-day practices of the work of ministry as senior pastors. The research questions explored the synergy and grit of how endurance and perseverance granted these men to become long-tenured pastors. Pastoring is not for the faint of heart; it takes boldness, courage, and trust in God, knowing you are called to complete such an assignment. It further explored the innate abilities and talents these men exhibited and implemented in their ministries to succeed.

The research consisted of seven pastors selected from across the country, all African American males, ages ranging from forty-two years to seventy-two years of age. The information was gathered by asking each of them the same questions to gather all the facts and data for this research design.

Review of Findings

The participants have been pastors for ten-plus years. The pastors are all senior pastors who have shown the discipline, tenacity, and resilience to successfully serve and reach the long tenure to become successful in their ministries. Resilience is defined according to Dekker's research as "The ability to thrive, mature and increase competence in the face of adverse circumstances or obstacles" (2011, 68). He further defines resilience as "the process of overcoming the negative effects of risk exposure, coping successfully with traumatic experiences, and avoiding the negative trajectories associated with risk" (Dekker 2011, 68).

The characteristics of these men have been proven by their calling, respect in their communities, and their good standing that is aligned with the principles and standards of the Church of God in Christ. The thematic outcome of this dissertation during this investigation answered the questions and depicted the picture of the why and how these pastors made it through the challenges and their calling and love for the ministry, the congregation they served, and the desire to conquer every test and trial that comes along with ministry. Prayer, servanthood, success, and making a difference in the lives of men and women who gather and follow these leaders weekly with their attendance and support. "It is the discipline of prayer that brings us into the deepest and highest work of the human spirit. Real prayer is life creating and life-changing" (Johnson, Hall, Daniels, and Herndon 2019, 310).

Servanthood was a guiding force that led these men to stand and move forward in the work of their ministries. The research of service depicted what it looks like to be servants in the work of ministry. "Clergy who thrive are those who have obtained success or prosperity throughout their careers through a variety of factors that may include a consistent desire to serve God and lead His people, the ability to reflect upon and learn from important experiences in ministry, and a focus on maintaining self-care and adequate support systems" (Bledsoe and Sutterlund 2015, 50).

Serving God is the ultimate of servitude, but it cannot be done without serving the congregation. These pastors heard the call of God. One of the participants stated, "Of course, at the same time you understand the responsibility of that call in terms of preparing yourself as a disciple of Jesus Christ in the real world; not just saying it but living that kind of life that glorifies and exalts him, lifts him ultimately" (interview with participant B, 2020). There is a lot of self-reflection over the years. The self-reflection affords them the ability to weigh out the pros and cons of the ministry and service they have given to the people of God. Therefore, it is without question or doubt that having the mind and heart of Christ is the epitome of being a good servant and pastor. "The King will reply, 'Truly I tell you, whatever you did for one of the least of these brothers and sisters of mine, you did it for me'" (Matthew 25:40 NIV).

"More than any other single way, the grace of humility is worked into our lives through the discipline of service" (Johnson, Hall, Daniels, and Herndon 2019, 317). Pastors don't walk into ministry, and everything falls into place overnight. As one participant stated, "The ministry needed structure, a path that kept me grounded and close to God both naturally and spiritually." This took discipline. One has to recognize what will make or break a ministry. The humility and integrity of senior pastors in the Church of God in Christ are admirable qualities that were seen in these pastors. It was further noted their service was not predicated on the size of their congregations. The sizes of their churches varied from small to large, and each of them gave the same selfless sacrifice and heart by serving their congregations. The sizes of their congregations may garner them different levels of financial income, but that was never an issue, or they made an indication of not wanting to serve based on their economical social statuses. A participant stated. "I don't ever want to put finances above God, because I know God can provide but I do acknowledge the fact having finances help you expand some things, increase what you're offering the reach of what you are doing" (interview with participant D, 2020). These men humbly and graciously kept something close to their hearts—a towel. "As the cross is the sign of submission, so the towel is the sign of service" (Johnson, Hall, Daniels, and Herndon 2019, 316).

Success is a driving element in the content of this dissertation. While many pastors walk away from ministry, give up serving, or no longer have the fortitude and strength to lead, these pastors pulled it out and made it happen. One participant expressed a bold and courageous statement as to why he has remained at the level of ministry God has called him to. "I think for me it is to understand where God is moving, where he is calling me to, and then finding myself there. That guarantees me number one that I am in the will of God. And if you are in the will of God you cannot fail" (interview with participant G, 2020). This does not sound like a pastor who has any intention of walking away or giving up the ministry he has been appointed to serve.

Many men in pastor roles before them were successful. They expressed the other pastors in ministry they admired, respected, and sought mentoring and guidance from. A participant shared, "I did have a connection with people before that had known me and seen me helped me, so it kind of helped me and open my mind to this whole concept of mentoring, and listening and being shaped and molded by the experience of others" (interview with participants D, 2020). It takes being a good follower to become a good leader. Someone who has walked this path and lived this experience as a pastor is by far one of the best and most important people to take sound advice or counsel from. This was rightfully shown in the lives of these pastors. Safe and wise counsel was mentioned in various interviews with these men. "The growth of the Church of God in Christ could, in a real sense, be in our pioneering generation and in succeeding generations" (Johnson, Hall, Daniels, and Herndon 2019, 311).

Making a difference ultimately is what each of these men desired to see in the lives of the men and women they teach, feed through the Word of God, preach the Gospel of Jesus Christ to, and all the other elements that are part of the ministry. It is not a one-man show but is an all-out expression of yielding, surrendering, and helping. "The role of the pastor comes with great responsibility. The work entailed in this field must be executed with a clear understanding of what all comes along with the role. There is something known as ministry satisfaction. A minister's job satisfaction or dissatisfaction is largely an artifact of his relative ability to fulfill the roles and perform the functions of the ministry as he perceives it" (Powell 2009, 235). A responsible leader accepts this role and all that comes along with it. Good accountability, good stewardship, and solid leadership are paramount. A satisfied leader has no intention of bailing out or walking away from his responsibility. The ministries of the senior pastors in this research have stood the test of times. There was a challenge in one of the participants' early roles in ministry. A ministry he was appointed to had gone through five or six pastors. He was asked to take the leadership of the church. In his words, "'Sure, I will it try it.' So I did, stayed there for three and a half years, my wife and I commuted; one Sunday morning they gave me a letter and said, 'You're fired!'" (interview with participant, B, 2020). As the research revealed, everything that may come along with the role of a pastor is not always what one hopes for. This participant felt like a failure and didn't think ministry was going to work; however, through this moment, he rose to the occasion and has been serving more than forty years in ministry.

Pastors have to come alongside the members who are hurting, searching, and asking questions to survive. "Your success in the ministry to which God has called and assigned you will be greatly enhanced as you attend to the need to perfect your spiritual disciplines and formation" (Johnson, Hall, Daniels, and Herndon 2019, 311).

Significance of Research

Gathering data from the senior pastors of the Church of God in Christ was a journey I was eager to take on as the role of a researcher because gathering data is important to have an interpretation of valuable and reliable research. As a graduate-level student, selecting men of various levels of education helped make the research more relatable and compatible with the peers of the many pastors serving this great church. Their academic standings ranged from high school to having a PhD. One participant shared, "Being that I am part of a denomination that does not require seminary training, it does not value seminary training like other denominations, mainline denominations" (interview with participant E, 2020). The men for this research went beyond the call of ministry to achieve academic accolades. This finding alone is a strong indicator that being self-motivated, eager to excel, and going beyond the call of duty are great attributes in being a successful and resilient pastor. The participant with the high school diploma stated, "Education affected the ministry for me in this vein, my training came from reading and studying God's word, and following leadership" (interview with participant A, 2020). It is not the means or level of education that makes the individual; it is the heart and tenacity to have a willingness and desire to learn and improve the calling as a pastor. One thing for certain is with the literature and material for study in the Church of God in Christ, you will find this scripture somewhere on the cover or in educational training forums: "Study to show thyself approved unto God, a workman that needeth not to be ashamed, rightly dividing the word of truth" (2 Timothy 2:15 KJV).

The research further captured this significant statement: "Pastors in a word have a highly visible leadership role" (Rowold 2008). Transformational leaders can inspire followers to go beyond their expected levels of commitment and contribution (Rowold 2008). This comes through by the leaders' modeling of task-related values and the commitment the leaders have toward their organization

(Rowold 2008). It is with this style of leadership leaders are inspired to keep excelling and climbing for greater results and identifiable results.

Previous Research

During this research, the discipline of prayer was an important factor for the successful outcome of pastors. "Putting prayer at the top of the list to maintain a strong healthy spiritual life" (Steiner 2017). A prayer life with reading the Word of God keeps men in ministry grounded and focused. It is helpful to implement spiritual disciplines, including fasting, devotions, worship, exercise, and the like. Every leader needs a foundation; therefore, prayer is very much a foundational characteristic of success in ministry.

Prayer was the most mentioned spiritual discipline expressed by the participants of this research. As phenomenological research uncovers the lived experience of an individual, I searched for what these men had in common, being that each of them had the same level of responsibility. Many of the disciplines founded in the Church of God in Christ are very much the same in most of the churches, though there will be various functions of administration that each may carry out.

I found value in the way one of the participants emphasized the importance of organizing and engaging in the work of ministry. "For me, I think organizing the church that I serve in such a way that I could fulfill my assignment." This is a good example to show that with the commonalities, there are independent differences for each of them.

Contribution to Others

I chose men forty years or older. Men in this age group have experienced the highs and lows that come with ministry but can move forward with a sense of urgency and commitment. One should not be a novice when assuming the role of a senior pastor. It comes with a life that has been dedicated to God to pursue the honored assignment of a pastor. The Church of God in Christ is a well-seasoned church that embraces fasting along with prayer. One of the participants expressed his success came through consecration. It is setting oneself apart to yield the heart, mind, body, and soul to God. It is not a fly-by-night vocation. Along with the maturity and soberness of heart for the men who participated in this research, it helped shape and mold the example for other pastors coming behind them to follow. The qualification of being in good standing with the church was a key indicator to even participate in this research. Having good standing made the conversation more engaging and relatable.

There are levels of degree before a person is promoted to the ranks of pastor. The journey begins as a minister, an ordained elder. Once a man is ordained, he can be appointed to the office of a pastor by the jurisdictional bishop of the organization.

The Church of God in Christ has indeed appointed some great men to serve and lead this great church. One of the questions for this research addressed the significance of being ordained. Ordination is not afforded to just anyone; these persons must be recommended and selected to have the hands of bishops placed on them as an affirmation of their calling as pastors. In the words of one participant, "I think being ordained in the Church of God in Christ is so significant to me because it is the organization that transformed my life, the lives of my entire family" (interview with participant E, 2020). "It gave me an identity and to be validated within an organization that I see as a family and who taught me the tenets of my faith; it's just an honor and to have been sanctioned not only by the church, by the man who was my spiritual father who ordained me was just an invaluable experience" (interview with participant E, 2020).

On the acknowledgment of ordination, these words placed greater emphasis on its importance and significance. "The reason ordination is important it is not exclusively from a denominational perspective but of the validation, authorization, authenticity of the call, because at the end of the day it matters who lays hands on you. Ordination says you have been tested, tried, vetted, and these men and leaders of great reputation and those who have been anointed themselves are sanctioning you" (interview with participant G, 2020). What a prestigious blessing to receive from the leadership of the Church of God in Christ.

Sharing What Works

One of the highlights of this research was to establish the successful retention and longitude of pastors serving in ministry. From previous studies, it has been stated, "Perseverance goes a long way in supporting one another in ministry simply for the fact it is not a one-man function but a corporate one" (Emlet 2017). Ministry requires giving of one's self—therefore, to lead healthily and productively develop a rhythm of life and protect it well (Steiner 2017).

A direct focus on the success of the pastors serving in the Church of God in Christ was driven by the fact that it takes personality to be a leader who interacts with a congregation on a regular basis. There is a myriad of personalities displayed by the men in the Bible serving in leadership roles. Some are successful, and others are not. Successful pastoral ministry has many sectors that must come through in the style and manner a pastor chooses to display. The various styles of these pastors came through in the personal interviews. There were moments of smiles, laughter, a pause, a reflection as to why they shared the responses from the questions. This made it very personal and more relatable. Their personalities complemented each of their leadership styles as senior pastors.

Furthermore, the research also addressed being relational as a leader and one who was trustworthy. "Relational leadership brings about influence from the vein that is built on personal trust" (Young and Firmin 2014). Trust is not something anyone should assume; it must be earned. "Relating to people is important, they have to see you as a real person, and you have to speak to them in their real-world" (Young and Firmin 2014, 5). The longevity of the tenures of these pastors was evident. The trust that has been gained with the followers is a testament to the relationship and leadership each of them has given of themselves to be pastors.

Without question, servitude and gratitude affected the lives of these senior pastors time after time. The candid interviews with these senior pastors further exposed senior pastors serving in ministry who have a love and heart of ministry. This research provides a look into the resiliency and tenacity of serving in ministry with a successful long-term tenure.

Specific Participation Requirements

The pastors chosen for this research are forty years or older, which is the time many men in this denomination are given the charge to lead a congregation. Men at this age group have experienced the highs and lows that come with ministry but can move forward with a sense of urgency and commitment. There are levels of degree before a person is promoted to the ranks of the pastor. The journey begins as a minister, an ordained elder. Once a man is ordained, he can be appointed to the office of a pastor by the jurisdictional bishop of the organization. These men further served faithfully and in good standing with the Church of God in Christ. To become long tenured, one must standfast and be committed to the end. "If you faint in the day of adversity, your strength is small" (Proverbs 24:10 ESV).

There are no limitations for pastors to make their ministries flourish, expand, and grow, where the people will see and feel the interest and dedication needed to make a difference in the lives of the followers. "In many ways, pastors are already some of the most resilient humans on the planet" (Barna 2017, 156). It is comforting to note pastors are forever bearing in themselves resilience and purpose. "Always bearing about in the body of the dying of the Lord Jesus, that the life also of Jesus might be made manifest in our body" (2 Corinthians 4:10 KJV).

In the humanness of leadership, there can be leaks, breaks, and moments where giving up would seem to be acceptable, but when the hand of God has appointed you and given you an ultimate tasking, something else intercedes and reigns in the decision to persevere. "And he said to me, 'My grace is sufficient for you for power is perfected in weakness. Most gladly, therefore, I will rather boast about my weaknesses, so that the power of Christ may dwell in me … for when I am weak, then I am strong'" (2 Corinthians 12:9–10 NASB).

One takeaway from this study is that the blueprint for success is written in the Word of God, just as he commanded the servant Joshua. Joshua was known as Moses's minister, meaning he knew what servitude was about. "This book of the Law shall not depart from your mouth, but you shall meditate in it day and night, that you may observe to do according to all that is written in it. For then you will make your way prosperous, and then you will have good success" (Joshua 1:1 NKJV). Pastors' mandate is to feed the flock of God with the Word of God, and in so doing, everyone benefits. The second point is the importance and necessity of having a resilience embedded in your heart when you yield to God's call. A very wise man shared with the congregation he served for twenty-four years a passage of scripture that stays in my spirit. He became the emeritus leader; he was a long-tenured pastor who is known today as the founder of the ministry where I serve. "Therefore, my beloved brethren, be ye steadfast, unmovable, always abounding in the work of the Lord, forasmuch as ye know that your labor is not in vain in the Lord" (1 Corinthians 15: 58 KJV). That's resilience at its finest.

Recommendations for Future Research

The direct benefits participants should expect to receive from taking part in this study are sharing your experiences that will be a valuable resource reference for future senior pastors. The average congregational size of most ministries on a Sunday morning is approximately eighty people. Many congregations in the Church of God in Christ come in various sizes. It is important to note, "The pastor is the primary leader in a local congregation. His/her role in the dynamics of the church organization may vary depending upon size, resources, and structure" (Johnson, Hall, Daniels, and Herndon 2019, 343). Research of this magnitude gives all pastors equal and level knowledge and a breadth of information to inspire and motivate them to become the leaders they have been called to be. Senior pastors have earned this great role of leadership for the years of labor and sacrifice they all have made. The Church of God in Christ has more than three thousand pastors who would benefit from research to reinforce and give great credence and credibility to remain faithful and dedicated to giving of acts of service to God.

Conclusion of Research

In the work of ministry serving in the Church of God in Christ, the research captured four themes from the investigation of seven pastors: prayer, servanthood, success, and making a difference. All of these areas helped these men maintain resiliency and provided direct focus when handling the challenges and engagement of the lived experiences as they served and led the people of God in their ministry. For a new pastor to walk into the job as a pastor, he wants to be able to step into the work with assurance, confidence, and clarity of what success and resilience look like in the Church of God in Christ. Mentorship from seasoned, mature, successful pastors is the mechanism to provide such an undertaking. The biblical principle of mentoring is well described in the writings of Paul. "But as for you, speak the things which are fitting for sound doctrine. Older men are to be temperate, dignified, sensible, sound in faith, in love, in perseverance" (Titus 2:1–2 NASB). He further addresses the conduct of young men. "Likewise urge the young men to be sensible. In all things show yourself to be an example of good deeds, with purity in doctrine, dignified. Sound in speech which is beyond reproach, so that the opponent will be put to shame, having nothing bad to say about us" (Titus 2:6–8 NASB). Gifting and modeling the behavior makes the work of ministry effective and an appealing, smooth transition to step into a pasture to feed the flock of God. "The Lord calls and qualifies leadership gifts such as apostles, prophets, evangelist, pastors, and teachers. There are distinct responsibilities for each leadership gifting" (Johnson, Hall, Daniels, and Herndon, 337–338).

Final Summary

Improved learning is a result of the resiliency and successful leadership of pastors serving in ministry. This study is worth doing simply because it addresses the roles, day-to-day taskings, and involvement of pastors who serve in the Church of God in Christ that have been successful and achieved the honor of becoming senior pastors. Their resolve, tenacity, and abilities to navigate the waters of ministry that can be challenging have proved that the work of ministry can be achieved with great success. The potential benefit to society is to share a learning outcome for future pastors to enter into this field with strength and confidence. The direct benefits participants should expect to receive from taking part in this study are sharing their experiences that will be a valuable resource for future senior pastors.

Appendix A

Interview Questions

1. What made you have the assurance you were called of God for ministry?

   a. Confirmation of others
   b. Specific vision from God
   c. Burning desire
   d. Other

2. How has education affected your calling as a pastor?

   a. Hunger to expand my spiritual awareness
   b. Challenged me to learn with more passion and commitment
   c. Opened my worldview of ministry and the study of God's Word
   d. Other

3. What sparked the passion in you to enter into ministry to seek the role of senior pastor?

   a. The commitment to be a true follower of Christ
   b. To see the kingdom of God expanded, reaching souls
   c. Making a difference in Christendom with a servant's heart
   d. Other

4. How do you define success in ministry and as a professional?

    a. Fruitfulness
    b. Growth in the knowledge of Christ
    c. Making disciples of men
    d. Other

5. Why is being ordained important to you in ministry?

    a. Respect of the hierarchy of the organization of the Church of God in Christ
    b. Obedience to the will of God living a consecrated life
    c. An honor to follow in the steps of leaders who were before me who set a great example
    d. Other

6. What are the signs of ministry that provoked you to be successful?

    a. Taking the reins of ministry in a changing climate
    b. Having the opportunity to see something small evolve into something great
    c. When others said it could not be done or would not succeed
    d. Other

7. What infrastructures did you put in place to help you stay the task in ministry both naturally and spiritually?

    a. Prayer services
    b. Solid educational ministries with Bible study, Sunday school, and other academic classes
    c. Influential and anointed music ministry
    d. Other

8. How important is it to establish an inner circle of other pastors in your circle of ministry?

   a. Having a trusted friend and confidant
   b. Sharing the burden of ministry
   c. Good accountability
   d. Other

9. What preparations have you made for serving in the role of a senior pastor?

   a. Educational goals
   b. Self-study
   c. Mentorship with trusted and respected leaders
   d. Other

10. How did you navigate challenging moments in your ministry?

    a. Prayer life
    b. Resilience and grit to press onward in spite of the circumstances
    c. Hiding the Word of God close to the heart
    d. Other

11. How important is family life for you as a pastor?

    a. Meaningful to have immediate family to help in ministering
    b. Helpful in having someone to be a sense of support and strength
    c. Modeling the example written in the Word of God for husband and wives
    d. Other

12. How necessary are finances to establishing ministry?

   a. Instrumental to do great exploits in the kingdom of God
   b. Vital and important to expand the work of ministries
   c. Meaningful and commensurate with the level of involvement rendered by the leader
   d. Other

Appendix B

Participants' Interview Transcripts

Participant A

Participant A serves as a pastor who has stood in the ranks of a shepherd for thirty-six years as its senior pastor. He is a father, husband, grandfather, and, more importantly, a shepherd who, in his own words, "I tested God, like Gideon," as he heeded the call to successfully serve in this vocation faithfully for God. At the age of sixty-two, he leads with the strength and commitment to be the leader his congregation welcomes him to be. Here's the intimate conversation conducted for this research:

> What made you have the assurance you were called of God for ministry?

> The assurance for me that I was called of God for ministry came with several factors for me. I respected the confirmation of others, and in my own space, I had a vision from God. More importantly for me, I tested God, like the character of Gideon.

> How has education affected your calling as a pastor?

My educational background and training came from reading and studying God's Word and following leadership.

What sparked the passion in you to enter into ministry and seek the role of the senior pastor?

I always felt I had a passion for ministry and as the role of a senior pastor I was committed to being a true follower of Christ, my love for souls was to see the kingdom of God expanded. It was further important for me to make a difference in God's kingdom working and serving with a servant's heart. The final analysis for me; God would not take no for an answer.

How do you define success in ministry and being a professional?

Success in ministry is defined with four key components, fruitfulness, growth in the knowledge of Christ, making disciples of men, with the biggest factor, satisfaction in knowing that I am pleasing God.

Why is being ordained important to you in ministry?

In the church of God in Christ being ordained is a key role for pastors serving in ministry. It was important for me solely because of its obedience to the will of God by living a consecrated life. It is also an honor to follow the steps of the leaders who were before me who set a great example. To see the ministry I served to become successful was crucial.

What are the signs of ministry that provoked you to be successful?

I was provoked to be successful because I had the opportunity to see something small evolve into something great and I had a past, God did not hold that against me!

What infrastructures did you put in place to help you stay the task in ministry both naturally and spiritually?

The ministry needed structure, a path that kept me grounded and close to God both naturally and spiritually. Prayer services were important. With my training, I found Bible study, Sunday school, and other academic classes relevant to the success of the ministry. As a musical person, I love anointed music ministry. Mentoring is important. I searched out and found other successful leaders and used their stories and experience to build upon.

How does establishing an inner circle of other pastors in your circle of ministry help you?

Having an inner circle of other pastors is important for my relationship with other pastors. A trusted friend or confidant is warranted, having a counterpart to share the burden of ministry, it provides good accountability and I find strength in fellowship.

What preparations have you made to serve in the role of a senior pastor?

My preparation to serve in the role of a senior pastor came mostly by self-study, mentorship with trusted and respected leaders. Lastly, the support of family has been my greatest encouragement.

How did you navigate through challenging moments in your ministry?

There is no getting away from challenging moments. I navigated through these moments with prayer life, hiding the Word of God close to my heart, resilience, and grit to press onward despite the circumstances. To be clear, always knowing within my heart, that I am called by God.

How important is family life for you as a pastor?

Family life is very meaningful having an immediate family to help in ministry. You need someone to provide you with a sense of support and strength. I love modeling the behavior of being a husband, having a wife as a great example from the Word of God.

How necessary are finances to establishing ministry?

Ministry requires finances to survive. It is vital and important to expand the work of ministries. I follow as close as I can to Matthew 6:33, "But seek ye first the kingdom of God and his righteousness; and all these things shall be added unto you."

Participant B

Participant B serves as the senior pastor of the midsized congregation he leads with more than forty years of experience. He is a loving husband, father, and grandfather who takes family to heart in the great tasking to lead a local congregation. One of the most memorable moments was when he shared the words one of his daughters said to him: "'Dad, can I be a member of your church?' I was like, 'What? You are already a member of my church.' She said, 'No, I want to be like everybody else. I want to be able to come into your office and talk to you like all the other members do.' Man, that blew me away. I mean I just, I didn't know what to say." Pastors give much of their lives to the family of God. He immediately took note of his own daughter's feelings and continues to meet the needs of home first and then his church family. Here's the open and heartfelt interview conducted with this awesome leader:

What made you have the assurance you were called of God for ministry?

> Well, I think first of all to even receive a call at all you have to be saved. You first have to have some kind of personal relationship with Christ yourself. Of course, at the same time you understand the responsibility of that call in terms of preparing yourself as a disciple of Jesus Christ in the real world, not just saying it but living that kind of life that glorifies and exalts him, lifts him up ultimately. For me, I really didn't have a lot of personal confirmation from other people. My confirmation came from God himself. I did not want to be a minister, did not want to preach, that was not in my bloodline. Amos said, "I was neither a prophet nor the son of a prophet" (Amos 7:14 NIV), so was my dad. In fact, my father wasn't even saved. So that

was not in my thoughts or intentions I had no real desire to do that, but I had to wrestle with God. I had to literally fight with God about ministry because I didn't want to do it. So I ultimately found myself, we were in a very high service one night, I think it might have been on a Friday night, and the spirit of the Lord was high and I found myself up in the pulpit. So that was my confirmation because I knew that was not where I wanted to be. That was a real confirmation for me. So then of course, after I entered into the ministry other people were kind of encouraging me and that kind of thing.

How has education affected your calling as a pastor?

You know years ago in Memphis during the last time of J.O. Patterson, the presiding bishop of the church and he made a statement that, "You can't teach what you don't know and you can't lead where you don't go." That stuck with me I guess over forty years ago. That stuck with me how to really understand how relevant Christian education is if you are going to be a leader. You can never stop learning, never stop growing you will never stop developing. It is a lifetime process. Never quit. There is no goal you can reach and say, "OK I have finally arrived." That doesn't happen if you are a leader. You are constantly growing, constantly developing, constantly evolving into all that God wants you to be. So education, the more education you can get, the more effective you be as a leader. You learn the skills, you learn how to understand the people, understand what it is that God has called you to do. So education is very important for that process. It equips you with personal skills, decision-making skills, organizational skills all of those kinds of things you are going to need if you are going to be an effective leader.

What sparked the passion in you to enter into ministry and seek the role of the senior pastor?

Well, probably all of those. Like I said earlier, I didn't want to be a preacher. I didn't feel qualified. I didn't feel like I knew enough to be a preacher because the one's I had observed were men who were educated, very refined men, and I didn't think I fit that role, I didn't fit the mode. I didn't want to go there. So God just kind of grabbed me and kind of jumped over a whole lot of other people and got to me. Threw me in the lion's den. That was not my intention. An opportunity came in the late seventy's in the life of the late Robert L. Chapman a church in Cleveland that came open. Nobody wanted to pastor that church. They had gone through five or six pastors already. Nobody wanted to take that church so he asked me. Being a young and adventurous type guy I said, "Sure I will give it a try." So I did, stayed there for three and half years, my wife and I commuted, one Sunday morning they gave me a letter and said, "You're fired." I thought at that time I was a failure, it wasn't going to work. I asked God to give me some direction and he did. He opened up a door that was back in 1981 and the rest is history. God has been moving ever since.

How do you define success in ministry and being a professional?

I was going to ask what did you mean by professional? In the sense of is it what we do as men and women what we do as a career, a vocation in life, in your craft, or being an expert in what you do? Professional development and spiritual growth are absolutely for success in ministry. You cannot be stagnant, you have to work at being all you can be and being the best you can be as it relates to leadership and that is an everyday ongoing process you are working constantly to improve who you are as a man or a woman of God. So you do whatever it is you have to do and use whatever tools you can use to make available for yourself to be the very best version of yourself that you can be. That is constant work. Success is a lot of time we think trying to reach a goal and once we reach that goal we say, "Now I'm successful." But success is not so much reaching a goal. Success is not so much reaching a goal. You can climb on the top of a building but if you are on the wrong building you are not successful. Being successful is really fulfilling the assignment you have been given by God. When you fulfill that assignment then you are successful because it is only at that point that God can say, "Well done, good and faithful servant."

Why is being ordained important to you in ministry?

Actually, ordination really wasn't important to me. I remained a minister for seven years. The only reason I got ordained my predecessor came to me, "Don't you think it's time to be ordained?" So I said, "Well, if you think so," so I was ordained. In my mind, God had already ordained me, called me to do what he wanted me to do. Understanding our church structure there were some things I could not do unless I had ordination papers from the organization itself. So ordination in that respect was important.

What are the signs of ministry that provoked you to be successful?

My military experience. I went into the military as a minister. I met hundreds of guys who were also ministers from different parts of the country. In my mind, at the time these guys were much further ahead in the ministry than I was. Just watching them, listening to them, hearing them, some of them had been to seminary and other places of higher learning and I had none of that. Watching these young men doing what they were doing it provoked me. I said to myself, "I got to do something." So that led me to seek for greater understanding, a more in-depth understanding of God's Word, and God's purpose. It then led me to buy books. At that time we didn't have any kind of educational arm in the church, it was just developing so we didn't have a great arm at that time so we bought books, invested in my ministry because of those young men of what I had seen and heard of those young men they inspired me so it pushed me to take myself to a higher level.

What infrastructures did you put in place to help you stay the task in ministry both naturally and spiritually?

I was a Sunday school buff. I loved Sunday school. One of the mothers at that time gave me a book. I think the name of it was Holbert Story of the Bible, it was something like that. In that book was information that was not in the Bible. So I had answers to questions that other young people in my age group didn't have so Sunday school for me it was exciting because I could ask those questions nobody had the answer but me. I enjoyed Sunday school, that was something I really enjoyed and that intensified my wanting to learn more and develop more. The Sunday school part of it at that time we had YPWW which was Young People Willing Workers and we were involved in that heavily. We had a great small group of young people who met every week for Bible study, for prayer, or fellowship engagement. One of the mothers of our church had us over every week. Every week would go over to her house for prayer, Bible study, fun, and games and eat. That relationship, in fact, most of those young people are still in the church today. The kind of relationship that we had going on back then that kept us in church kept us grounded and helped to solidify our relationship with Christ. It was just a great time back then. We are missing that now that we don't have the opportunity to do that kind of fellowship and have those kinds of relationships on an on-going basis. It was something that solidified us, kept us all in church, kept us strong we did a lot of praying, a lot of things of that sort, to keep us strong trying to keep this flesh under subjection as young people and those were the things that kept us going. There was a young friend of mine, his name was Walt Williams. We were just young people trying to do something for God and we developed a ministry for young people. We had a city-wide youth choir. Every Friday night we would take our young people to a pizza place, buy all the pizza, bought potato chips, we laughed, talked and the name of that program was Off the Street. It was designed to get young people off the streets on Friday nights to bring them together to fellowship. We did a thing when we all dressed up in tuxedos, we all went out to a luxurious place and had dinner with our little girlfriends. Those were the kinds of things we did to keep all of us solidified and keep us in the church. We kept something going on. We were not bored at all.

How does establishing an inner circle of other pastors in your circle of ministry help you?

Wow, you know pastors in the position that they're in, working with people on a daily basis take a lot out of them, it drains them of their energy, emotionally, mentally, physically because they are on call twenty-four hours. It is unfortunate that the horizontal relationship that inner circle you just mentioned that people we can go to we can trust, people we can feel safe around, people we know who will give us an honest report of ourselves and that's for me is missing. I don't know a lot of pastors who have an inner circle where they can feel safe. Where they can say, "You know I am dealing with an issue I have a problem. Will you pray for me to help me get through this?" and do it in a level of confidentiality that they can trust. That is very few and far between. For me, you know you get kind of leery because you don't have that kind of person you can talk to and pour out to and that's unfortunate. I don't know of a lot of our pastors have that, I'm sure it would be helpful if we had that kind of ministry going on particular today because of stress, so much strain, trying to do things that we do and sometimes you just need somebody to talk to. As a matter of fact, I was talking to someone, we had a conference call today a Zoom Call with the bishops, one of the bishops said, "You know maybe this is just something we need to do on regular basis, just talk." Just deal with the issues all of us are facing. To understand you are not the only one dealing with this. You are not the only one going through this. You're not the only one trying to figure all this out. You don't feel like you're out there by yourself and no one understands what's going on. So we need that kind of relationship at a much greater level than we see it going on today. It is unfortunate, we can't find that safe place in the church. There are things that some pastors are dealing with. If they would tell somebody things that's really going on the inside, they would be shut out, excommunicated. Being in the position you are in, "How could you be doing that?" We don't have that kind of place where we can go. I know some people take for example; T. D. Jakes, has his I don't know if he still has his mega-conference or not but I know people who have gone to those kinds of conferences just to release themselves and deliver themselves and free themselves from things because whoever they are talking to they will probably never see them again so they are free to relieve themselves so they are able to get that shame or burden off of them so they can be liberated to be free to do what God wants them to do. Unfortunately, we don't have that. We need that ministry.

What preparations have you made to serve in the role of a senior pastor?

I have done all those things, especially the educational aspect of it. I kind of I guess it is my thought, years ago when I first entered the ministry. An old Baptist, not an old Baptist minister he said, "Kimbrough, you need to go to school." I'm like at that time I'm like man I am Church of God in Christ, I'm Holy Ghost Filled, Fire Baptized, I don't need to go to school. I told him I can just preach the gospel and let the Holy Ghost do the rest. I don't need school. Little did I know, I needed school. Eventually a little late, but eventually I did go and I did acquire a degree and of course you know I'm working on another one now. But going to school is one thing I did to prepare myself watching and observing other men who are in a position of leadership what they are doing and how they were doing it. Doing a lot of investigation as to what other ministries are doing as it relates to ministry, trying to prepare someone to succeed me which makes sure that what whatever point in time you know God says, "OK it's time to come home," there will be somebody in place that can take the ministry on and all the work done prior to myself in the life of the late Bishop Mack E. Jonas and the life of the late bishop Robert L. Chapman, all of that work won't be in vain. Because I would have provided someone, prepared someone, positioned someone to take over, and keep that ministry going until it's time for them to go off the scene and God sends somebody else.

How did you navigate through challenging moments in your ministry?

There again all of those things as I mentioned earlier, the first pastorate I had, I was young. I'm sure I made a lot of mistakes but after that incident, I felt like a failure, I felt defeated. But I wasn't ready to quit. I knew in my heart in my mind and I knew that God had called me to ministry and because I knew that and I was assured of that I wasn't ready to quit. I inquired of God and prayed that he opens up a door in which he did and he manifested himself in a way that was just incredible. My father got saved under my ministry. That was a highlight under my ministry. My brother-in-law got saved under my ministry, Pastor McIntyre. These were men who I looked up to, one was my dad the other my brother-in-law, neither one of them were churchmen. My father came to my revival. I did a two-week revival. The last night my wife invited my father to come and he said OK. He came the very last night of that two-week revival and gave his life to Christ. That night and he was my first deacon. A month later, Pastor McIntyre came in, gave his heart to God, he was my second deacon. God moved like that. In the middle of winter, in December, snowing a lot and we had a revival that started off was supposed to be one week ended up being a month and a half. We were packing the place out, snow was on the ground a foot deep, God was moving, people were healed, people were delivered, and it was that kind of manifestation of God's power in my life, in my ministry, that let me know you can make it. Those challenging moments but yet God manifested himself and let me know I'm not gone leave you. I brought you out here to bring you in.

How important is family life for you as a pastor?

You can't say too much about the family. I am a very fortunate man because when I was coming along they taught us, God, church, and everything else comes along after that. My, all of my time all of my free time, vacation time, and all that kind of stuff was given to the church. We never went on vacation. We went to Memphis for the national call meeting, we went to the national convocation, and we took our kids to all of those events, but a vacation for a family in that respect we didn't know that because we were I was so committed to the church and its teachings and its doctoral tenets and one day my wife told me she says, "You're losing your sons." I'm like, what are you talking about. She let me know your sons are growing up, they don't know who you are because you are never here. That rocked me. The thing that really got me the most was my daughter. She came to me one day and said, "Dad, can I be a member of your church?" I like, "What? You are already a member of my church." She said, "No, I want to be like everybody else. I want to be able to come into your office and talk to you. Like all the other members do." Man, that blew me away. I mean I just, I didn't know what to say. It shook me. I had to start prioritizing my family. Give my family time. Before I hadn't done that. I was fortunate that God because, in my ignorance, he blessed me. And allowed my family, my children to love the church, and love God and they are in the ministry now, and you know that, and it's because God honored my ignorance and my sacrifice to him. He knew what I was doing to him with a true heart to serve him so he blessed my effort. So my family is together, they are tight, my kids work in the church, they have ministries in the church, and it is just been a blessing to have them in the ministry that I oversee. It's incredible. We have a great family and I tell anybody that strong families make strong churches. If you don't have a strong family you are not going to have a strong church. That's just the way it is. Families are very important, and I tell young men now its God, then your family and you know, the church. I told a bishop not long ago, "Jesus died for the church, so I don't have to die for the church." Jesus did that two-thousand years ago, I learned that now. Take out more time with my family now than I use to do. Families are important, they are the foundational basis in what we do in ministry.

How necessary are finances to establishing ministry?

Since money is the medium of exchange on this planet, if you don't have any money you are not going to get very far, you are not going to do a whole lot as it relates to ministry. Ministry cost. We always say salvation is free and that's true but to do ministry it is going to cost you because there are so many things involved that especially in today's culture perhaps years ago they didn't worry about. Pastor was the pastor of the church, maybe his daughter was the secretary, maybe his son was the drummer and maybe his wife was something else, but today that is not the case. We have a staff, we have to worry about the secretary, we have custodians, got musicians, maintenance on buildings, the repair and upkeep and all these things, all that stuff cost money. Jesus in the Word of God spoke more about money more than he did anything else. It is unfortunate that for us money is almost a bad word. If you start talking about money in our church people start getting fidgety, nervous, and wonder, what are you doing with all that money? We trying to keep the church going is what we are trying to do. It just takes a lot of money to reach out, reach souls, support other missions on the other side of the world and particularly in our church we are involved with 102 churches in the world so you know sometimes we try to send something to support those ministries so all of that costs. Money is absolutely necessary if you are going to have an effective ongoing ministry. You can't get around it.

Participant C

Participant C serves as the senior pastor of a congregation he has led with the oversight bestowed upon him by God for fourteen years. At sixty years of age, he has taken his assignment to heart with diligence, commitment, and love for not only his devotion to his family but to the body of Christ he leads honorably. His passion as a senior pastor shined brightly from his own words during our conversation: "Having the passion to make a difference in someone's life for me there is nothing more rewarding when you hear someone say you were responsible for saving my life. And for me, that is like water on a seed. It just causes me to want to do more, take the ministry further, reach another soul." Here's the candid interview conducted with him for this research:

What made you have the assurance you were called of God for ministry?

> I'm going to answer all of the above. And with a footnote others, that burning desire, confirmation through others, also the call, I heard, but I kept hearing God. That's what really triggered everything. I kept hearing from him. It's like we're talking right now, I heard him and he would manifest himself in certain ways, sometimes in a dream, sometimes through others, but I just kept hearing him, so I would say that was the deciding factor.

How has education affected your calling as a pastor?

> I would say other, as for me, what education has done for me. I know that there is a calling and an anointing on my life. What that has done it has allowed it to go further, be advanced, enhanced. The anointing that God has given to me. I was thinking of a scripture where it says, God has given us the ability with the power to get wealth, he didn't particularly put wealth in our hands but I have given you the resource to go get. I look at education the same way. With ministry, we can desire all these things that we want but to take it to the next level in a lot of cases you need to take what God has given us or what he has made available and use it to advance.

What sparked the passion in you to enter into ministry and seek the role of the senior pastor?

I would say, mercy, can I answer all of them? Again, all of the above because truthfully I genuinely want to make a difference in someone's life. And as I mentioned earlier, I ran from it for a long time but I know that the anointing is on my life to make a difference you know, anointing comes from the Hebrew word, which means to smear, and when you can make a difference when you can take what God has given you and help others with it, that just drives me, it just absolutely drives me, but again, it was that call from God that told me to do this work, I didn't want to do this for myself.

How do you define success in ministry and being a professional?

What I'm all about is B. Making disciples of men. That was one of the well thee great commission by Jesus Christ. A lot of times that gets lost in the shuffle of everything that's going on but that was the great commission for us to make disciples of others, I would say B.

Why is being ordained important to you in ministry?

I would say, other. All those things could be or may be important, but from a natural standpoint being ordained, it helps doors to be opened for you, where without ordinarily being ordained some of those doors would be shut, closed. So this is an opportunity to take the ministry further than what it can go in certain areas having certain credentials.

What are the signs of ministry that provoked you to be successful?

I would say again, other. And I don't want to sound like a broken record, but that passion to make a difference in someone's life it for me there is nothing more rewarding when you hear someone say you were responsible for saving my life. And for me, that is like water on a seed. It just causes me to want to do more, take the ministry further, reach another soul. Go on another day regardless of whatever happens from a negative standpoint in my life when I hear, listen, you made a difference in my life, that in itself produces life in me. I was talking to a bishop the other day and I told him, that to be responsible for taking someone out of darkness into the light and what God gave me was right there as we were talking, God said, "There's life in the light. There is life in the light." To be an instrument God uses literally causes someone to live to walk in that light is just a passion.

What infrastructures did you put in place to help you stay the task in ministry both naturally and spiritually?

Again, I'm going to say all of those because the Sunday school, Bible studies, it helped me to get where I am. And again music, a lot of people don't realize and understand music, that sets the tone for the service for God to come in and move in like he does with his kind of glory. So, I'm going to say, all of the above in addition to all of those, the infrastructure which is basically the foundation is a genuine and sincere desire to walk close with God. Because so many times we are trying to build without hearing God. How solid can your foundation be if you are not really hearing God? All of the above.

How does establishing an inner circle of other pastors in your circle of ministry help you?

Again, all of the above. I truly believe that all of us especially as a pastor, we need someone to pour into us. We are always pouring out. I just made an illustration with my children that were all here, if I'm constantly pouring into someone and no one is pouring back into me, I'm empty, and before you know it when someone needs something from me I'm empty because I don't have nothing to give. So when you have that inner circle where you can confide in someone, trust in someone, that really does help and also the reason I said other I was listening I believe it was T. D. Jakes one time said something that sparked a thought with me. One of the reasons why I like to get with other pastors because they understand what I'm experiencing or going through. In addition to that, it gives me a sense of hearing something different, looking at it from a different perspective and if everyone I hang around are people like me, I would never get stronger in my weak areas. Because they're just like me. They think like I would, they digest everything like I do. So I would never get stronger in the areas I am weak because they are going to mirror everything I say and do. When you have that offset, that balance with someone different they may be stronger in the areas I am weak and help bring something to the table and areas they are weak might be stronger in a particular area and be able to so that's the reason I would say the other. I tried not to look at the questions, I wanted it to come from here, my heart.

What preparations have you made to serve in the role of a senior pastor?

All three of those, educational goals, mentorship, respect for others, all of that I would say would be my answer to that question.

How did you navigate through challenging moments in your ministry?

All of the above and other. I thank God for a prayer life because I truly don't see how a person can make it without a prayer life. God showed me something one time. I was at work talking to an employee and I asked her to do something for me. She was on the other side of the counter. She said, "I can't hear you." I said, "Well, come here." She started moving closer to me. My pitch wasn't any higher and I repeated myself and as she drew closer to me she heard me clear. That's what prayer life has done for me. As I draw closer to God when things really get rough and tough I have to hear God. I have to. This is not the time for me to start asking God for forgiveness, all this other stuff that sometimes can interfere with the connection, but my prayer life keeps me in tune with God all the time so when those trying times do come God gives me direction, he gives me hope, there is a scripture where he talks about, patience, experiences, the experience that gets me through those rough times because he tells me I brought you through that last year, so that gives me to experience what I'm going through now, so it gives me that hope, so that would be my answer to that plus the other.

How important is family life for you as a pastor?

I'm going to say all of the above again and other. I think this is the way I feel personally. I have scriptures to support it, it would take an hour. I truly believe if you have a family, I truly believe that is our first calling. And if we don't take care of our home according to scripture so I truly believe all of the above and others, when you have family involved, I thought about Myles Munroe, we talked about this before once that success without a successor is a failure. Success without a successor is a failure. If everything I have and know and I don't share it with my children, my children's children and I go to my grave how successful was I. And if I impart, whatever that is that means to me that is a success because it doesn't die if I die. Who better else than to pour into our family because generally speaking, they have the same spirit. Sometimes a different building but the same foundation.

How necessary are finances to establishing ministry?

I'm going to say all the above and other. Definitely all of the above because I've learned personally that you can be anointed, have friends, you need money to pay bills. You really do. For me when you get a plan and work it you get a little money on the side or saving it really feels good, takes a lot of pressure off you. Nothing worse than in ministry as a leader to have too much pressure on you. When you don't have money to pay bills, when you don't have money to see things, that's a lot pressure. And another area that I'm learning members man I don't care what size building you have, they want to see a progressive church. Every now and then, buy a new lamp. A floor mat, something. If you don't have any money you can't make that happen, so the people get disgruntled. Before you know it they're talking about leaving, what you're doing with my money, so on and so on.

Participant D

Participant D stands tall among the pastors interviewed during this research. At forty-nine years of age, he is a strong, courageous, and hands-on leader with the community and at the forefront of all he does with his work in the kingdom of God. He has led the charge as a senior pastor for twenty-four years. He is a husband and father who has earned a PhD, with an unyielding passion for education to make one better in doing the work of ministry. His words about how education has affected his calling and work as a pastor follow: "It has challenged me, to try to learn the word better, yes it impacted my worldview, but also for me it afforded me the chance to as I often say, to bring language, and connect my passion for justice and community effort with the church." Here's the conversation conducted for this research:

What made you have the assurance you were called of God for ministry?

> It was, it was, confirmation from God. That was very much encouraged, my mother, pushed that. I was trying to get her because my grandfather was a pastor, so I was trying to get my mother to tell me something like they prophesied it when you were a kid, but she was like, "Naw, baby, you need to know for yourself." These black folks in church will try to make everybody a preacher. You have to know for yourself. It was from God.

How has education affected your calling as a pastor?

> I'd probably say other. Because I think it is all of those. It has challenged me, to try the learn the Word better, yes it impacted my worldview, but for me it afforded me the chance to as I often say, to bring language, and connect my passion for justice and community effort with the church. With the purpose and call for ministry. Because I was raised in the church, my parents never directedly connected their social actions, their social activism to faith. They just said, "This is the right thing to do." It was through the academy that I actually got exposed to liberation theology, black theology, feminism, womanistic theology, and learned there was language to the fact that the church is called to be involved in the community and fight for justice, not just to jump and shout, be sanctified and in the church.

What sparked the passion in you to enter into ministry and seek the role of the senior pastor?

For me, it was making a difference in Christendom. Because like I said, I felt God calling, I also saw this opportunity as I have always believed we tried to do all these years intentionally blend Pentecostalism, social justice to me it was an opportunity to at that time I thought to develop and build a church that a COGIC church I had not seen before. I have since seen them as I have learned and met more people. I thought this was going to be totally different from what I thought COGIC, of what I had been exposed to and a chance to expand the kingdom and kind of do ministry in what I thought was a biblically faith way, different than what I was exposed to.

How do you define success in ministry and being a professional?

For me, I'd probably say other. Because of the fact I see success as fulfilling what God has called you to do and what that might look might look different based upon who you are and where you are and what you are actually called to do. I do believe it's that whole idea of expanding the kingdom making more disciples, but I look at it as its kind of like a holistic approach so you are seeing people come to the kingdom, you're seeing people develop and grow as believers, you're seeing people hopefully moving to finding their purpose, filling their purpose and to also hopefully having some type of impact upon the community or part of the world. I don't only see ministry success is not only individualistic or in the sense of solely about numbers but also what type of impact are you having that may not necessarily be quantifiable, in the traditional aspect of doc, how many you running, what you looking at that type of thing.

Why is being ordained important to you in ministry?

I probably, once again go with other, not because the options you give are all good, cause there is that sense of hierarchy, being connected to something bigger than you that I don't want to say validate affirm but acknowledges some way, God has called you and that you know met some standards, so that's important I think the primary reason I say other is cause technically when I started Nehemiah, I started and was not ordained yet. So I actually started as a minister and I got ordained January, and I got ordained in the local church in July, then the jurisdiction in August, so there was a time in which, well, I'm talking too much, but anyway. There was a time in which I had that whole being ordained was man's thing didn't mean anything if God hadn't anointed you. But I have since then also learned that there is value in the affirmation, and the hands being laid on, that there is a connection beyond yourself. That the ordination connects you with the tradition of your church, but also the ministry lineage that has been passed on. That is not anything to be frowned upon, look down upon. Look down upon even if there were people I thought growing up were ordained and didn't demonstrate anointing, were not seemingly gifted and I thought it was better to be gifted and anointed than being ordained, but as I realized it didn't have to be a bifurcation of the two, you could be anointed and gifted and ordained. There is benefit to it. A little complex answer.

What are the signs of ministry that provoked you to be successful?

Wow, another other. Because it was kind of a mixture of something small blossoming into something bigger, successful, but then also I did have some people early on that said it wouldn't work, that I was too young and that I shouldn't have done it. It was interesting, I even had college students who actually joined the church when we started but part of them being college students running their mouths before, they were like, "He's a good preacher and teacher and does Bible study but he's too young, he should be working with somebody else instead of starting his own church." And then some of them actually came and joined as members while they were at school, some stayed, it was for me it's been kind of a mixture so I would say other.

What infrastructures did you put in place to help you stay the task in ministry both naturally and spiritually?

It would probably be the educational ministries. That has probably been one of the bedrocks that we focused on, whether that is Bible study, try to do solid preaching, training classes, youth ministry so yes for us, really it's been trying to anchor things on the Word, trying to help people grow in their understanding of the Word and how to understand and hopefully apply it.

How does establishing an inner circle of other pastors in your circle of ministry help you?

Other, because I think it's all of those for me, it's having those people you can trust, those you can be accountable with, and also people who will understand, yes other. God knows it can be lonesome out here, if you don't intentionally develop that circle that's going to help keep you accountable that can be trusted and keep pushing you.

What preparations have you made to serve in the role of a senior pastor?

Again I would say, other. Because I probably have done all of those. The educational piece, the self-study, mentor thing, I've done it but it is probably been much more over the past ten to twelve years prior to that it was a little different for me because I think I was always trying to find it. After all, I really felt I did not have a spiritual father, per se. I know the pastor that I started preaching under is still the pastor at my home church. Good guy, we were never close and I was never even before when we had a previous pastor this guy was an evangelist and he would come do revivals. I was never even as a kid highly impressed with his preaching, it wasn't bad, it was just, it didn't resonate with me a lot. So although I respected him as a pastor, there was not really a closer relationship so I really for years, before I started, I sounded like Moses being on the backside of the mountain, I was young, little less wise, I would make comments like, "Everything I learned was on the backside of the mountain." I don't need, I remember telling one pastor, when I first moved to North Carolina, I told him, "I'm just being upfront with you. I'm not looking for a spiritual father, I never had one, God taught me what I needed to know, I'm here at your church because God told me I needed to be." When I look back at it now I was twenty-four, bold running your mouth, talking to this man, I'm like wow, that was extreme. But over time I kind of recognized and realize that my pastor was not necessarily my spiritual father, that I did have a connection with people before that had known me and seen me helped me so it kind of helped me and open my mind to this whole concept of mentoring, being mentored, and listening and being shaped and molded by the experiences of others. That's my long answer for others.

How did you navigate through challenging moments in your ministry?

It's other. Doing all of those. I mean, yes, prayer life, holding to the Word, what I believe God said in his Word, what I believe God said to me but I have, I look back at it now there was still a high level of resilience, and grit that at the moment I didn't'. I realize quite as much. I think I saw it as this is me pushing through it because of my prayer life, my reliance on what God has said in his written Word and proclaimed Word and didn't I think over time I've come to realize that grit and resilience is key to helping those things stick together. It's not solely grit and resilience because that cuts out God but without it; I've seen many people not make it through challenges that I think they could have and I thought they were people of the Word, people of prayer, so I think yeah, prayer life, locked in the Word, grit and resilience all worked together for my numerous challenging moments.

How important is family life for you as a pastor?

The second one, having family there for support. That is really key for me. One thing I have always tried to raise up I was the one called to pastor not my family. But I do know that puts a burden on them, but I have tried not to overburden my children or my wife with regards to that. So having them there for support, that's been key.

How necessary are finances to establishing ministry?

Vital and the second one expanding it is true you have to have finances to do ministry. But I don't ever try not to put finances above God, because I know God can provide but I do acknowledge the fact having finances does help you expand some things, increase what you're offering the reach of what you're doing. That is vitally important we have to be careful not to raise money higher than God. Because God will provide rather that's stretching, whether that's sending somebody to give, however it works. I think even though we are trusting God to provide we can't get somewhere and think finances are not important and not doing something with them.

Participant E

Participant E is the youngest senior pastor who took part in this research at the age of forty-two years. A force to be reckoned with, he is a leader who became pastor by his eagerness to work in the role as a supply pastor, which changed the course of his work to what he has become today. He is a young husband, a father who is making a difference in the kingdom of God. He says, "God used that opportunity to confirm for me that I was called to the pastoral ministry because if he had not set me up for it, I would not be pastoring." Here's the candid interview for this research:

What made you have the assurance you were called of God for ministry?

> For me, I'm going to say, first of all, the environment I was raised in. I grew up in a home that was Christ-centered, ministry-focused, so I think I developed an appetite and a desire for ministry early on in my life. I began ministry when I was a toddler and I think as I began to grow, becoming older I began to connect my life experiences with the call to assist people, also had experienced some of the things that I and my family did. I felt my purpose on earth.

How has education affected your calling as a pastor?

> Education, being seminary trained, really gave me a greater understanding of my call. I think it helped me to define the purpose of my assignment. And it assisted me in digging deep within myself. Learning what was in me to give and it helped me to know how to execute the ministry God had given me.

What sparked the passion in you to enter into ministry and seek the role of the senior pastor?

Honestly, I didn't seek to be a senior pastor, I had gone to seminary and I needed an opportunity to do ministry, being that I am a part of a denomination that does not require seminary training, it does not value seminary training like other denominations, mainline denominations and so I ended up getting an opportunity to come to Milwaukee to work and while I was here, I was offered an opportunity to be a supply minister. Because I supplied for a church, when it was time for them to vote on their candidate, I was not one, I was requested, and as a write-in, I won the vote. God used that opportunity to really confirm for me that I was called to the pastoral ministry because if he had not set me up for it, I would not be pastoring.

How do you define success in ministry and being a professional?

I define success as impacting lives. I think when you have a vision you execute that vision to completion and it has impacted one or more lives I believe that's a success. To me, success is completing your assignment. Whatever that is and so, that's how I measure it. I've grown to that because at times in ministry I looked at it as what I thought it should be, what others were doing and thought I should have that, but I've learned that whatever it is that God has assigned to your hand and whoever it is he has put in your path, to influence; when you do that, you are successful.

Why is being ordained important to you in ministry?

I think being ordained in the Church of God in Christ is so significant to me because it is the organization that transformed the life, the lives of my entire family. It gave me an identity and to be validated within an organization that I see as a family and who taught me the tenets of my faith it's just a high honor and to have been sanctioned not only by the church, by the man who was my spiritual father who ordained me was just an invaluable experience. Secondly, I understand the necessity of ordination in order to execute fully all duties of my assignment as a clergyman.

What are the signs of ministry that provoked you to be successful?

The signs for me once again, back to the third question the sign for me when I see that person's lives are being changed, people testifying of how the ministry I provided impacted them, changed their lives, changed their family's lives it provokes me, encourages me to do more.

What infrastructures did you put in place to help you stay the task in ministry both naturally and spiritually?

I'm just going to say prayer. Prayer has been my foundation. It has been, our ministry has been built on prayer from the time I started I committed to leading the church in prayer at a dedicated time every single week; I prayed with the church. When

I first started, I pastored two churches but I prayed with that first church every week. So from then until now, fifteen years I've done this. There have been seasons like now where I pray every day with the church. There have also been seasons that I prayed three times a day with the church. Prayer; it's it.

How does establishing an inner circle of other pastors in your circle of ministry help you?

I would say having a trusted confidant and sharing the burden of ministry those both; I could elaborate on that but I believe those answers are really acceptable.

What preparations have you made to serve in the role of a senior pastor?

I would say all the above. Education, not just my seminary training, I have a masters of divinity, not only that, being mentored by seasoned pastors and other education like leadership development trainings and pastoral leadership conferences.

How did you navigate through challenging moments in your ministry?

It was all the above, all the above, in addition to having a support system of people outside of my local church and even city that loved me and were there for me through every up and down in ministry. I could not have made it without a support system. A healthy support system, no way.

How important is family life for you as a pastor?

It's very important. I am very much committed to my family, very much committed to trying to find the balance time-wise, spending time letting them know is important, but also I want my family to know God. Ministry for me starts at home.

How necessary are finances to establishing ministry?

I think all of the above. It's very important. You cannot execute without the capacity to do certain things, finance is important to fund the vision, and finances being in order meticulously will make your ministry attractive for more funding to do what you need to do. The call of God on our lives needs to be financed.

Participant F

Participant F has served as senior pastor for nineteen years with the congregation he was blessed to serve after the death of the late Bishop Robert L. Chapman. A husband, father, as well as an anointed musical pastor, he is gifted to preach and sing. The question was asked, "What sparked the passion in you to enter into the ministry and seek the role of the senior pastor?" He stated, "I want to say making a difference in Christendom with a servant's heart. My story is I succeeded a great man. And I was his heir apparently, and with that, it propelled me into the pastorship." This is a great example of how the succession of a leader is made in the church of God in Christ during one of the most transitional moments in ministry. Here's the interview:

What made you have the assurance you were called of God for ministry?

I would say it was a specific vision from God. It was something I ran from, I didn't want, didn't even desire. It was absolutely God.

How has education affected your calling as a pastor?

I want to say the second one, I think it has enhanced my passion. In all thy getting, get an understanding. If we are not able to rightly divide the Word of God, if we are not taught from the Word of God and how to execute it; we do ourselves a disservice. I think it is very imperative that we have an education.

What sparked the passion in you to enter into ministry and seek the role of the senior pastor?

I want to say making a difference in Christendom with a servant's heart. My story is I succeeded a great man. And I was his heir apparently, and with that, it propelled me into the pastorship.

How do you define success in ministry and being a professional?

Do I have to pick one or can I use a couple? I would think that fruitfulness would be, that sticks in my heart, my mind, and my spirit. It's not the amount of congregants you have, it's the training, maturity, and the growth of the individuals that you serve. So I would think, making disciples those both when I heard the question that's what I was thinking.

Sometimes we look at numbers and I think about the scripture that God disciplined David for numbering the people. I think we have to be careful even in this pandemic that we are not so concerned with numbers but souls.

Why is being ordained important to you in ministry?

I'm going to say the second one. It would be the obedience to Christ. I'm Church of God in Christ through and through. I'm not going to take that away, but I don't think it's because of the organization. My allegiance is to the Lord first and then to the organization. I will probably get in trouble with that. Because my father was a Church of God in Christ pastor, my grandfather was a Church of God in Christ elder, I have uncles who were ordained in the church of God in Christ, biologically, then I served dad Chapman. It's nice to be ordained but it wasn't because of the organization it was because God had called me.

What are the signs of ministry that provoked you to be successful?

I would think it would be provoking to servanthood. I think the Lord empowered me to minister because I was a servant. Because I was a servant I think that's how God did it. It was a God thing, it wasn't anything, I was just as happy being on the piano, playing over the choir, happy in that realm. It wasn't something I craved or desired. I believe it was always on my life. God had shown me a vision years before that I would pastor and the church would be red.

I never even realized it that because at the time I went to be associate pastor we didn't even have red pews, we had brown chairs. So the Lord showed me years later that that's what he was calling me to do.

What infrastructures did you put in place to help you stay the task in ministry both naturally and spiritually?

I'll say two things. The Lord gave me through Bishop Chapman three mentors as a young person. One was Drew Sheard, Eric Slack, the other one was Joel Lyles. He told those three people to take care of my son. That was in a leadership conference probably, I was just an associate pastor, it was many years ago. Those three men have kept me grounded. They have kept me, I have been able to sound off to them, I've been able to, and it's good because we all need that. That was good for me. That would be the first part and in the second part, I would think that the music ministry has been very impactful in my life. Very, very impactful. It has paid, I had a member of our church who said, "Pastor, you can pray, sing, and preach." And for different reformations that's big. You know in the Baptist church they want you to be able to sing, pray, and preach. So I would think that has been a very impactful foundation in my life.

How does establishing an inner circle of other pastors in your circle of ministry help you?

I'm going to say the very first one of accountability. I think we have to be accountable to one another. I can call a Pastor Terence Hayes and vent, be able to share. I think we need that because pastoral ministry is unlike any other. Out of all the gifts that are in Ephesians pastoring stands out. I think that accountability would be first and you do need a circle, you can't tell everybody what you're going through, there is a burden of pastoral ministry that only pastors can understand. So I would say the very first one is accountability.

What preparations have you made to serve in the role of a senior pastor?

I'm going to say it would be educational and also mentorship. I have been to a few conferences and what has really blessed me and I haven't been in the last couple of years or so, but Bishop Jakes has a conference that I was able to attend and I still to this day can glean from the notes that I took in those three-day conferences. It was a small one it was the Gideon one, that is held at the beginning of the year and I'm telling you even to this day I will go back in my I-pad and I really hunger and thirst for more education its different being bi-vocational and dealing with our everyday lives, our families, but I do hunger for great knowledge and to be around people that soar in the educational realm.

How did you navigate through challenging moments in your ministry?

I want to say first of all it was consecration. The first one and the third one are praying and scripture coupled together. I've had some challenging moments. This is my nineteenth year. There was a time we had a great exodus because of other people, because of other situations and all, but the Lord gave us resilience and now we have doubled back and we are thriving. So I would have to say prayer and scripture because God had to have something in you for something to come out. Absolutely being resilient in ministry and knowing that I'm not going to give up.

How important is family life for you as a pastor?

I think it is very meaningful. I've watched my family and I took a tip from Bishop Chapman who didn't do a lot of things with his sons. To the point, he always said "James, make sure your family is close to you." I take it very seriously family life, balance is very important to me. My wife has been with me in ministry. My oldest daughter has done things in the ministry and she is not in church, but she does all our graphics, she's working on our web design, and this past Summer the Lord has allowed her and my other daughter they did all our women bathrooms, put flooring down, the whole nine. Painted it and so it's a blessing for me because we need our families with us. My wife, when I beg her and push her to preach she will preach for me. I tell her she was called before I was called. She is a woman of God that can proclaim the Word of God. So I think it is very important, its pivotal, now. I think we have to be careful because we need their support, we need them undergirding us, they're prayers because they see what everybody else doesn't see. So I think it is critical.

How necessary are finances to establishing ministry?

It's vital for kingdom work. It's very essential we can't do ministry without money. The finances, the Lord has to give us the wisdom of how we are to execute. Have you retired yet? So you understand bi-vocational of how we have poured out of our funds into the ministry for it to be instrumental and for other people to rally around us; this beautiful edifice that you all have to pour in resources, so it is very important, it is for the kingdom, it is for the ministry to be expanding, for exposure, for you to be able to bring people in that can assist you and help you in ministry so I think it's vital.

Participant G

Participant G steps into the ranks of pastorship as the game changer of a generation who is looking for a leader to lead by example and take the work of ministry to heart day one on the job. At forty-two, he has climbed the ranks from pastor to the role of a bishop in the Church of God in Christ. He hit the ground running, being a father, husband, and the senior pastor who keeps setting the precedence for greater works to come. Humility is a strong characteristic in this leader. During the interview, he stated, "Having a heart of servanthood is very significant in understanding the role of a senior pastor. As we all understand Jesus said, 'Whoever is greatest among you be the servant of all.' Accepting that role and responsibility as a pastor most definitely there must have been a heart matter." Here's the interview:

What made you have the assurance you were called of God for ministry?

I really think it may be a mixture of all of those, I don't know if that's an appropriate answer. I think if my memory serves me correctly, it mentions a confirmation by God, it says vision from God, I think that could be conclusive of you know just the leading, the prompting of the spirit of God and a desire to please God. So I think it's probably not one of a specific answer it could be a hybrid or mixture of all of them. That really brought me to the point of understanding what the call of God was for me in my life.

How has education affected your calling as a pastor?

Same thing again. I think all of them are very critical that as a minister and leader that we are to open up ourselves for opportunities for development, empowerment, for training, and if that is in a formal educational perspective, most definitely and I value education very significantly.

What sparked the passion in you to enter into ministry and seek the role of the senior pastor?

It's almost like again, a mixture, but I will say I think having a heart of servanthood is very significant in understanding the role as a senior pastor. As we all understand Jesus said, whoever is greatest among you be the servant of all. Accepting that role and responsibility as a pastor most definitely there must have been a heart matter. Notwithstanding, ultimately the call of God being convinced, convicted that this is the will of God for our lives. So being motivated by his assurance of this purpose he has given us and then just understanding what the true call of a pastor is and aligning ourselves with that.

How do you define success in ministry and being a professional?

For me, success in ministry reflects a ministry that is fulfilling of the purpose of the assignment and the call of the ministry that God has given them. I know there is a blanket or corporate mission of the Lord's church but all of us individually as pastors and the churches we serve I believe there is a unique call that God may have for us and we find ourselves pursuing that vision and pursuing that mission and when we do that to me that's the definition of success.

Why is being ordained important to you in ministry?

I wish I could choose some of those options you have there but if I may go with other, I would have to say the reason ordination is important it is not exclusively from a denominational perspective but of the validation, authorization, authenticity of the call because at the end of the day it matters who lays hands on you. Ordination is not about a certificate. It is not about regalia or the garb that one has the opportunity to wear, but ordination says you have been tested, tried, vetted, and these men and leaders of great reputation and those who have been anointed themselves are sanctioning you. So you are not out there as an island, out there coming from nowhere. There is a validation of who you are.

I think that goes all the way back to the biblical days of the New Testament church we see in the Book of Acts the scripture would say, "The Holy Ghost separated unto himself Paul and Barnabas," and yet the apostles had to come and lay hands on them. So that was somewhat of an ordination, an authorization. So that is the significance to me, even as a pastor, as a Bishop, you see that the presiding Bishop, General Board lays hands on that bishop so it's apostolic succession and someone laid hands on this case, Bishop Charles Blake. Whoever laid hands on Bishop Charles Blake there's a link going back to Bishop Mason and we believe this link goes all the way back to Jesus Christ, so somehow and another all of us who are in the ordained ministry, in our case the Church of God in Christ should point back to Jesus Christ.

What are the signs of ministry that provoked you to be successful?

I guess this is another other. I think that for me it is to understand where God is moving, where he is calling me to, and then finding myself there. That guarantees me that number one that I am in the will of God. And if you are in the will of God you cannot fail. You may experience failure here and there but ultimately you will see the kind of success so knowing that God was calling for this or calling me there, to do this or that, it brought a motivation to pour my all into it because I knew the ultimate outcome would be successful. It would cause to the other points you raised or options that were there when some may have said when it could not be done, I understood what God was saying or resilient in the process and also seeing something well really you start with nothing and it becomes something. But at the base of it all the foundation is the fact that we are where God is. Many times pastors if they are not careful they will go somewhere, do something, start something, and then ask God to come along and bless it. As opposed to finding where God is moving what he is saying and doing. And to get with that we try to get God to come along with our program.

What infrastructures did you put in place to help you stay the task in ministry both naturally and spiritually?

For me I think really organizing the church that I serve in such a way that I could fulfill my assignment so that means developing a structure that supported the vision, ministry, that supported the vision through various ministries, auxiliaries, there's a very strategic organization, in turn, administration, financial administration, and taking all of those components organizing them and placing people where they perhaps have a calling or their best strength is manifested and then on the personal side my naturally perspective I guess you can say with spirituality is really managing my time and balancing giving that you know pastoring, family first of all husband and father, pastor, bishop, working with our national church and just in the community, things that we are doing, really putting myself on a time schedule daily as well as in addition to building an infrastructure organizationally, administratively at the local level. There's a group I have I lean on for the jurisdiction. And there's a group I lean on for the national AIM convention. I try not to cross-pollinate, if I can say it like that these people are specific to those areas. I have an administrator who handles my personal calendar, I have a church secretary that handles exclusively everything rather for Citadel, so on and so forth. And so just building different infrastructures and I know that requires me to be able to go into those different circles and then put on a different hat just depend on what the circumstances are. I don't know if that answered your question.

How does establishing an inner circle of other pastors in your circle of ministry help you?

I want to say good accountability, that could mean a number of things. Because it speaks of friendship they become a confidant but also a sounding board, that accountability piece. Also, reflects someone that's connected to you being able to be in touch with the feelings of your infirmities. Offer whether its spiritual, prayerful, counseling support throughout the life as my role as a pastor and minister so I value pastoral relationships pretty good.

What preparations have you made to serve in the role of a senior pastor?

I can say all the above. All of that great mixture. Want to make sure that nothing is left out of that. But I will say all of the above if that could be an option.

How did you navigate through challenging moments in your ministry?

I want to say A and C. I want to add in there seeking wise counsel. I want to go back to the other question that was asked about of having certain individuals that share the burden of ministry with you. There are various challenges an individual can face in ministry and building a church, etcetera. Just not being so proudful to say I don't know when I need help and it may be sometimes relative to things that are not so spiritual, it may be administratively, financially, and it could be spiritual it could be dealing with problematic members. Dealing with something you dealing with personally, just depending on the context and situation. Just having someone as well that you can connect with. In addition, have your personal prayer life and having that resilience and all of that, and the Word of God associated with it.

How important is family life for you as a pastor?

What is the importance of the family life for a pastor? To me, that's a pastors first ministry. I could be wrong but I do not believe any individual ought to attempt to pastor, or minister, especially in this context of pastoral ministry. If their family life is not where it needs to be. The Bible speaks of how can one manage, rule the house of God, and not able to manage the affairs of his own home. The qualifications of a bishop and a deacon are one that rules his own house well, and that his children, family reflects of the ministry he or she has projected. And so family life really is the foundation it is important and of I know I'm not speaking in terms of some of the options that were there regardless if whether they are involved in terms of helping now it is a blessing to have their support, help, and involvement you want that. I think that will happen but foundationally I think that the first ministry is home, the wife, the children, ensuring you are the priest, the prophet, the provider of your home. If you are unsuccessful in being the priest, provider, protector of your home, then how are you going to do that as a pastor? A pastor is a priest, prophet, protector, and provider of a local congregation. I say that is the primary first ministry of any pastor.

How necessary are finances to establishing ministry?

If I can answer it like this, I know I just jacked up your whole survey of the research process. I'm not sure who came up with this but I subscribe to it. "People plus money equal ministry. The context I believe of that and suggest that in this world there is a matter of exchange and resources of finances is critical to operating and conducting ministry and it goes back to what I was saying earlier about family dynamics, the idea of finances and money is so critical for a leader, number one he must have integrity, and know-how to manage and manage well in terms of the financial perspective and it is very necessary that funds and monies are available to enhance and move forward the work of God. What is critical is especially when you're starting out you have limited resources and the significance is you be found faithful at managing what you have until God blesses you with more. Manage it well, just because you don't have what the next pastor has down the street doesn't mean that what you have is not as significant it's just the season and process and the level you are in and understand you cannot further the work of God without the financial support and so I guess to piggyback on some of the options that are there it is instrumental to do great exploits, it's not the only thing that is needed but it is instrumental and it is important to expand the work of God. The Bible says and the Lord gave to every one of those servants according to their several abilities. Which means their capacity to be able to manage at that level. I will say this and stop. There was a superintendent here in Memphis who said this all the time, "You can tell more about a man of how he manages his money than you can by how he shouts and dance, preach, and speaks in tongues." Money speaks and says a lot. Jesus said, "Wherever your heart is there will be your treasure also." I think is very significant that financial support means and management and be part of the pastors' leadership in ministry.

Appendix C

Recruitment Letter

26 August 2020

Terence O. Hayes Sr.
Faith Deliverance Church of God in Christ
xxx xxx
Dayton OH, xxxxx

Participant A
xxxxxxx Ave
Cleveland, OH 44106

Dear Pastor xxxx,

As a graduate student in the School of Behavioral Sciences at Liberty University, I am conducting research as part of the requirements for a doctoral degree in Community Care and Counseling, with a cognate in Pastoral Care and Counseling. The purpose of my research is to explore the traits necessary to becoming a successful pastor within the Church of God in Christ and I am writing to invite eligible participants to join my study.

Participants must be male, 18 years of age or older, African American, and currently senior pastors in the Church of God in Christ with at least 10 years of experience in that role. Participants, if willing, will be asked to participate in either a telephonic or in-person audio-recorded interview and to review their interview transcripts for accuracy. It should take approximately 30–45 minutes to complete the interview. The interview transcripts will be emailed to participants within 7 days of the interview, will take approximately 15–20 minutes to review, and will need to be returned by email to me within 7–10 days of receiving the transcripts. Names and other identifying information will be requested as part of this study, but the information will remain confidential.

In order to determine your eligibility to participate in this study, please call me at (xxx) xxx-xxxx.

A consent document will be emailed to you if you are found eligible to participate in this study. The consent document contains additional information about my research. Please sign the consent form by typing your name and date on the form and return it to me either by email or by mail prior to the interview.

Participants will be mailed a $50 VISA gift card for their participation in the study.

Sincerely,

Terence O. Hayes Sr., MA
Senior Pastor

APPENDIX D

Consent Document

Title of the Project: A Phenomenological Investigation of the Resilience and Success of African American Pastors Serving in the Church of God in Christ.

Principal Investigator: Terence O. Hayes Sr., MA, Liberty University Doctoral Student

Invitation to Be Part of a Research Study

You are invited to participate in a research study. To participate, you must be male, 18 years of age or older, African American, and currently a senior pastor in the Church of God in Christ with at least 10 years of experience in that role. Served faithfully and in good standing with the Church of God in Christ. Taking part in this research project is voluntary.

Please take time to read this entire form and ask questions before deciding whether to take part in this research project.

What is the study about and why is it being done?

The purpose of the study is to explore the traits necessary to becoming a successful pastor within the Church of God in Christ.

What will happen if you take part in this study?

If you agree to be in this study, I would ask you to do the following things:

1. Participate in either a telephonic or in-person audio-recorded interview. This will take 30-45 minutes to complete.
2. Review the interview transcript for accuracy. The interview transcript will be emailed to you within 7 days of the interview, will take approximately 15-20 minutes to review, and will need to be returned by email to the researcher within 7-10 days of receiving the transcript.

How could you or others benefit from this study?

Participants should not expect to receive a direct benefit from taking part in this study.

Benefits to society include improved pastoral resiliency and leadership within the Church of God in Christ.

What risks might you experience from being in this study?

The risks involved in this study are minimal, which means they are equal to the risks you would encounter in everyday life.

How will personal information be protected?

The records of this study will be kept private. Published reports will not include any information that will make it possible to identify a subject. Research records will be stored securely, and only the researcher will have access to the records. Data collected from you may be shared for use in future research studies or with other researchers. If data collected from you is shared, any information that could identify you, if applicable, will be removed before the data is shared.

- Participant responses will be kept confidential through the use of pseudonyms. Interviews will be conducted in a location where others will not easily overhear the conversation.
- Data will be stored on a password-locked computer and in a locked filing cabinet. The data may be used in future presentations. After three years, all electronic records will be deleted and all paper copies will be shredded.
- Interviews will be recorded and transcribed. Recordings will be stored on a password-locked computer for three years and then erased. Only the researcher will have access to these recordings.

How will you be compensated for being part of the study?

Participants will be compensated for participating in this study. A VISA gift card payment of $50 will be provided for your participation. The gift card will be mailed to you upon the completion of this study.

Is study participation voluntary?

Participation in this study is voluntary. Your decision whether to participate will not affect your current or future relations with Liberty University. If you decide to participate, you are free to not answer any question or withdraw at any time without affecting those relationships.

What should you do if you decide to withdraw from the study?

If you choose to withdraw from the study, please contact the researcher at the email address or phone number included in the next paragraph. Should you choose to withdraw, data collected from you will be destroyed immediately and will not be included in this study.

Whom do you contact if you have questions or concerns about the study?

The researcher conducting this study is Terence O. Hayes, Sr. You may ask any questions you have now. If you have questions later, **you are encouraged** to contact him at (937) xxx-xxxx or xxxxx@ liberty.edu. You may also contact the researcher's faculty sponsor, David Hirschman, at xxxxx@liberty.edu.

Whom do you contact if you have questions about your rights as a research participant?

If you have any questions or concerns regarding this study and would like to talk to someone other than the researcher, **you are encouraged** to contact the Institutional Review Board, 1971 University Blvd., Green Hall Ste. 2845, Lynchburg, VA 24515 or email at irb@liberty.edu.

Your Consent

By signing this document, you are agreeing to be in this study. Make sure you understand what the study is about before you sign. You will be given a copy of this document for your records. The researcher will keep a copy with the study records. If you have any questions about the study after you sign this document, you can contact the researcher using the information provided above.

I have read and understood the above information. I have asked questions and have received answers. I consent to participate in the study.

☐ The researcher has my permission to audio-record me as part of my participation in this study.

_____   _____

Printed Subject Name   Signature & Date

Appendix E

IRB Approval Letter

LIBERTY UNIVERSITY.
INSTITUTIONAL REVIEW BOARD

Subject: IRB-FY20-21-49 - Initial: Initial - Exempt

Date: Wednesday, August 26, 2020 at 3:44:41 PM Eastern Daylight Time

From: irb@liberty.edu

To: Hirschman, David (Community Care and Counseling), Hayes, Terence

Attachments: ATT00001.png

August 26, 2020

Terence Hayes

David Hirschman

Re: IRB Exemption - IRB-FY20-21-49 A Phenomenological Investigation of the Resilience and Success of African-American Pastors Serving in the Church of God in Christ

Dear Terence Hayes, David Hirschman:

The Liberty University Institutional Review Board (IRB) has reviewed your application in accordance with the Office for Human Research Protections (OHRP) and Food and Drug Administration (FDA) regulations and finds your study to be exempt from further IRB review. This means you may begin your research with the data safeguarding methods mentioned in your approved application, and no further IRB oversight is required.

Your study falls under the following exemption category, which identifies specific situations in which human participants research is exempt from the policy set forth in 45 CFR 46:

101(b):

Category 2.(iii). Research that only includes interactions involving educational tests (cognitive, diagnostic, aptitude, achievement), survey procedures, interview procedures, or observation of public behavior (including visual or auditory recording) if at least one of the following criteria is met:

The information obtained is recorded by the investigator in such a manner that the identity of the human subjects can readily be ascertained, directly or through identifiers linked to the subjects, and an IRB conducts a limited IRB review to make the determination required by §46.111(a)(7).

Your stamped consent form can be found under the Attachments tab within the Submission Details section of your study on Cayuse

IRB. This form should be copied and used to gain the consent of your research participants. If you plan to provide your consent information electronically, the contents of the attached consent document should be made available without alteration.

Please note that this exemption only applies to your current research application, and any modifications to your protocol must be reported to the Liberty University IRB for verification of continued exemption status. You may report these changes by completing a modification submission through your Cayuse IRB account.

If you have any questions about this exemption or need assistance in determining whether possible modifications to your protocol would change your exemption status, please email us at irb@liberty.edu.

Sincerely,

G. Michele Baker, MA, CIP

Administrative Chair of Institutional Research

Research Ethics Office

BIBLIOGRAPHY

Abernethy, A., G. Grannum, C. Gordon, R. Williamson, and J. Currier. 2016. "The Pastors Empowerment Program: A Resilience Education Intervention to Prevent Clergy Burnout." *Spirituality in Clinical Practice* 3 (3): 175–86.

Adams, C., and M. Bloom. 2017. "Flourishing in Ministry: Wellbeing at Work in Helping Professions." *Journal of Psychology and Christianity* 36 (3): 254–59.

Adiprasetya, J. 2018. "Pastor as Friend: Reinterpreting Christian Leadership." Jakarta Theological Seminary. *Dialog, (57)* 1: 47-52

Barnard, L., Curry, J. (2011). The Relationship of Clergy in Burnout to Self-compassion and Other Personality Dimensions. *Pastoral Psychol*, 61, 149–163

Barna Group (2017). The State of Pastors. How Today's Faith Leaders are Navigating Life and Leadership in An Age of Complexity. Pepperdine University

Barton, K. (2017). Foundations for Ministry. *Pastoral Music, (41)* 2

Beaumont, S.M. Pastoral Psychol (2011) 60: 117. Pastoral Counseling Down Under: A Survey of Australian Clergy https://doi-org.ezproxy.liberty.edu/10.1007/s11089-010-0289-4

Berry, A., Francis, L., Rolph, J. & Rolph, P. (2012). Ministry and Stress: Listening to Anglican Clergy in Wales. *Pastoral Psychol* (2012) 61:165–178 DOI 10.1007/s11089-011-0388-x

Bledsoe, T., Setterlund, K. (2015). Thriving in Ministry: Exploring the Support Systems and Self-care Practices of Experienced Pastors. *The Journal of Family and Community Ministries, 28*

Bond, K. (2007). *A servant's Guide from a Servant's Heart. Ministry from A-z.* Bonded Music

Borling, D., LaSalle, L. (2018). Grit and Spiritual Learning. *Lutheran Education Journey, 34*

Braunack-Mayer, E. When Ministry Becomes a Yoke too Hard to Bear! [online]. *Lutheran Theological Journal,* Vol. 52, No. 1, May 2018: 16–19. Availability:

Bumgardner, L. (2015). Adventist Women Clergy: Their Call and Experiences. Part II. *The Journal of Applied Christian Leadership, 9*(2), 40–53. Retrieved from http://ezproxy.liberty.edu/login?url=https://search-proquest-com.ezproxy.liberty.edu/docview/1766243487?accountid=12085

Burns, Chapman, & Guthrie (2013). Resilient Ministry. What Pastors Told us About Surviving and Thriving. Downers Grove, IL: InterVarsity Press

Caffaerata, G. (2017). Respect, Challenges, and Stress Among Protestant Pastors Closing a Church: Structural and Identity Theory Perspectives. Pastoral Psychol (2017) 66:311–333 DOI 10.1007/s11089-016-0751-z

Capps, D. (2014). The Minister and Mental Illness. *Pastoral Psychol* (2014) 63:13–22 DOI 10.1007/s11089-012-0499-z

Carson, M. (2019). Resilient Readers: Spiritual Growth and the Bible. *Journal of European Baptist Studies. (19)*1

Carter, J. (2009). Transformational Leadership and Pastoral Leader Effectiveness. *Pastoral Psychol, 58,* 261–271

Cattich, J. (2012). Three Models of Clergy Systems: Analysis of Couple Processes and Spiritual Meaning. *Pastoral Psychol 61:*

Chandler, D. (2009). Pastoral Burnout and the Impact of Personal Spiritual Renewal, Rest-taking, and Support System Practices. Pastoral Psychol (2009) 58:273–287 DOI 10.1007/s11089-008-0184-4

Clinton, T., Pingleton, J., & Hindson, E. (2001). The Soul Care and Counsel Bible. Thomas Nelson

Clinton, T., Pingleton, J. (2017). *The struggle is Real. How to Care for Mental and Relational Health Needs in the Church*. Bloomington, IN: WestBow Press

Considine, T., Hollingdale, P., Neville, R. (2015). Social Work, Pastoral Care and Resilience. *Pastoral Care in Education, (33)*4, 214–219

Cooper, L., Bruce, J. Harman, M. & Boccaccini, M. (2009). Differentiated Styles of Attachment to God and Varying Religious Coping Efforts. Journal of Psychology and Theology, 37(2), 134–141

Corcoran, K., & Wellman, J. (2016). "People Forget He's Human" : Charismatic Leadership in Institutionalized Religion. *Sociology of Religion*: 77(4), 309–332

Corey, G. (2009). *Theory and Practice of Counseling and Psychotherapy.* 8th ed. Belmont, CA: Thomson Books/Cole

Davis, H. (2015). *The Christian Leadership Blueprint. 7 Principles for Building Some Great, Transformative, and Lasting*. Bush MultiMedia

Dekker, J. (2011). Resilience, Theology, and the Edification of Youth: Are We Missing a Perspective. *The Journal of Youth Ministry*

Dillen, A. (2012). The Resiliency of Children and Spirituality: A Practical Theological Reflection. *International Journal of Children's Spirituality, (17)*1, 61–75

Dillard, L. (2015). *Engineering Your Vision. Seven Principles for Obtaining Ultimate Success in Every Area of your Life*. Memphis, TN. Linwood Dillard Ministries

Doehring, C. (2015). Resilience as the Relational Ability to Spiritually Integrate Moral Stress *Pastoral Psychol, (64)*, 635–649

Dollhoff, E., Scheitle, C. (2013). Decline and Conflict: Causes and Consequences of Leadership transitions in Religious Congregations *Journal for the Scientific Study of Religion* (2013) 52(4):675–697

Doolittle, B. The Impact of Behaviors Upon Burnout Among Parish-Based Clergy. J Relig Health 49: 88–95

Elkington, R. (2013). Adversity in Pastoral Leadership: Are Pastors Leaving the Ministry in Record Numbers, and if so, Why? *Verum et Ecclesia* (34) 1 #821

Emlet, M. (2017). Persevering in Ministry. *JBC 31*(3), 17–34

Fallon, B., Rice, S. & Howie, J.W. (2013). Factors that Precipitate and Mitigate Crises in Ministry. *Pastoral Psychol* 62: 27–40

Feist, J., Feist, G., & Roberts, T. (2013). *Theories of Personality.* 8th ed., New York: McGraw Hill

Forney, D. (2010). A Calm in the Tempest: Developing Resilience in Religious Leaders. *Journal of Religious Leadership, 9*(1)

Foy, S., Mueller, C. (2018). Nourish the Soul or Damage the Body? Belief in the Connection Between Christian Moral Failure and Diminished Health. *Social Compass Vol. 65(2)* 247–262

Fredrick, T., Dunbar, S., Thai, Y. (2018). Burnout in Christian Perspective. *Pastoral Psychology, 67*: 267–276

Hall, T. (1997). The Personal Functioning of Pastors: A Review of Empirical Research with Implications for the Care of Pastors. *Journal of Psychology and Theology,* (25)2, 240–253

Harmon, B., Strayhorn, S., Webb, B., Herbert, J. (2018). Leading God's People: Perceptions of Influence Among African-American Pastors. *J Relig Health,* Vol 57, 1509–1523

Helms, E. Cheshire, K., N & Walters, A. I (2015). Construct Validity of the Masiach Burnout Inventory in Mental Health Workers: Differentiation from Traumatic Stress Disorders. *Archives of Business Research, 3*(6), 149–163

Heinrichs, G. (1993). Power and the pulpit: A Look into the Diversity of Ministerial Power. *Journal of Psychology and Theology,* (21) 2, 149–157

Heppner, P., Wampold, B., Owen, J., Thompson, M., Wang, K. (2016). *Research Design in Counseling.* 4th ed. Boston, MA: Cengage Learning

Jackson-Jordan, E. (2013). *Clergy Burnout and Resilience: A Review of the Literature.* Atlas

Johnson, A., Hall, D., Daniels, D., III, Herndon, A., (2019). *Church of God in Christ Ordination and Licensure Textbook. Memphis,* TN. Church of God in Christ Publishing House

Jones, L. (2018). Pastoral Power and the Promotion of Self-care. *Sociology of Health & Illness* Vol. 40 No. 6 2018 ISSN 0141-9889, pp. 988–1004doi: 10.1111/1467-9566.12736

Joynt, S., Dreyer, Y. (2013). Exodus of Clergy: A Practical Theological Grounded Theory Exploration of Hatfield Training Centre Trained Pastors. *HTS Teologiese Studies/Theological Studies 69* (1), Art. #1940, 9 pages

Joynt, S. (2019). The Cost of "Not Being Heard" and Clergy Retention. *Acta Theologica, (39)1:*110–134

Kinman, G., McFall, O., & Rodriguez, J. (2011). The Cost of Caring? Emotional Labour, Wellbeing and the Clergy. *Pastoral Psychol, 60:* 671–680

Lee, C. (2010). Dispositional Resiliency and Adjustment in Protestant Pastors: A Pilot Study. *Pastoral Psychol (59)* 631-640

Lindholm, G., Johnston, J., Dong, F. et al. Clergy Wellness: An Assessment of Perceived Barriers to Achieving Healthier Lifestyles. J Relig Health (2016) 55: 97. https://doi-org.ezproxy. liberty.edu/10.1007/s10943-014-9976-2

Louw, D.J., 2015, 'Compassion Fatigue: Spiritual Exhaustion and the Cost of Caring in the Pastoral Ministry. Towards a "Pastoral Diagnosis" in Caregiving', *HTS Teologiese Studies/ Theological Studies* 71(2), Art. #3032, 10 pages. http:// dx.doi.org/10.4102/ hts. v71i2.3032

Luciotti, R. (2019). Clergy Self-care. *International Journal of Choice Theory and Reality Therapy, 2*

Malphurs, A. (2013). Advanced Strategic Planning. A 21st-Century Model for Church and Ministry Leaders. Third ed. Grand Rapids, MI: Baker Publishing Group

Mattes, M. (2017). How to Cultivate Biblical, Confessional, Resilient, and Evangelistic Pastors. *Lutheran Forum*

Manala, M. (2010). A Triad of Pastoral Leadership for Congregational Health and Well-being: Leader, Manager and Servant in a Shared and Equipping Ministry, *HTS Teologiese Studies/Theological Studies 66 (2)*, Art. #875, 6 pages

Manen, M. (1997). Researching Lived Experience, 2nd edition. Human Science for an Action Sensitive Pedagogy. London & New York: Routledge Taylor & Francis Group

Manen, M. (2014). Phenomenology of Practice. Meaning-giving Methods in Phenomenological Research and Writing. New York, NY. Taylor & Francis

McGrath-Merkle, C. (2010). Gregory the Great's Metaphor of the Physician of the Heart As a Model for Pastoral Identity. *J Relog Health* 50:374–388.

McKenna, R., Eckard, K. (2009). Evaluating Pastoral Effectiveness: To Measure or Not to Measure. *Pastoral Psychol, 58*: 303–313

McKenna, R., Yost, P., & Boyd, T. (2007). Leadership Development and Clergy: Understanding the Events and Lessons that Shape Pastoral Leaders. *Journal of Psychology and Theology, (35) 3*

McKenna, R., Yost, P., & Boyd, T. (2007). Leadership Agility in Clergy: Understanding the Personal Strategies and Situational Factors that Enable Pastors to Learn from Experience. *Journal of Psychology and Theology, 35*(3)

McMinn, M., Lish, R., Trice, P., Root, A., Gilbert, N., Yap, A. (2005). Care for Pastors: Learning from Clergy and Their Spouses. *Pastoral Psychology, (53) 6*

Meek, K., McMinn, M., Brower, C., Burnett, T., McRay, Ramey, M., Swanson, D., & Villa, D. (2003). *Maintaining Personal Resiliency: Lessons Learned from Evangelical Protestant Clergy.* (31)4

Miner, M., Stirland, S. & Dowson, M. (2009). Orientation to the Demands of Ministry: Construct Validity and Relationship with Burnout. *Review of Religious Research*, Vol. 50, No. 4. 463–479

Moore, M. (2017). *Provisions for the Journey. A 31 Day Roadmap to Breakthroughs Through Fasting, Prayer, and Planning* Monee, IL: Keen Vision Publishing

Moustakas, C. (1994). *Phenomenological Research Methods.* London, New Delhi, SAGE publications

Muhammad, A. (2018). Heartcore. Effective Leadership Starts with a Servant's Heart. Dallas, TX: Heart Core Publishing

Muse, S., Love, M., & Christensen, K. Intensive Outpatient Therapy for Clergy Burnout: How

Ngamaba, K. (2014). Religious Leaders' Perceptions of their Emotional and Psychological Needs. *Mental Health, Religion & Culture, 17*(1), 62–78

Pickett, C., Barrett, J., Eriksson, C., Kabir, C. (2017). Social Networks among Ministry Relationships: Relational Capacity, Burnout, & Ministry Effectiveness. *Journal of Psychology & Theology,* 45(2), 92–105

Pitt, R. (2012). *Divine Callings. Understanding the Call to Ministry in Black Pentecostalism.* New York, New York University Press

Powell, D. (2009). Skilled and Satisfied: Research Findings Regarding Executive Pastors. *Christian Education Journal,* 6 (2)

Proeschold-Bell, Chongming Yang, Matthew Toth, Monica Corbitt Rivers and Kenneth Carder, Closeness to God Among those Doing God's Work: A Spiritual Well-being Measure for Clergy. *Journal of Religion and Health* Vol. 53, No. 3 (June 2014), pp. 878–894

Price, J. (2013). Undergraduate Perceptions of Vocational Calling into Missions and Ministry. *Missiology: An International Review. 41* (1), 87–96

Puls, T., Ludden, L., Freemyer, J. (2014). Authentic Leadership and its Relationship to Ministerial Effectiveness. *The Journal of Applied Christian Leadership, 8* (1)

Randall, K. (2013). Clergy burnout: Two Different Measures. *Pastoral Psychol, 62,* 333–341

Random House Unabridged Dictionary 2020 (n.d.) Citation. In *dictionary.com*

Reed, A. (2016). Rooted in Relationship: Longevity in Congregational Ministry. *Review and Expositor 113*(3), 303–314

Resane, T. (2014). Leadership for the Church: The Shepherd Model, *HTS Teologiese Studies/Theological Studies, 70* (1), Art. #2045, 6 pages

Resources and Support for Ministers and Pastoral Care, Inc. (2020)

Rodgerson, T., Piedmont, R. (1998). Assessing the Incremental Validity of the Religious Problem-Solving Scale in the Prediction of Clergy Burnout. *Journal for the Scientific Study of Religion*, Vol. 37, No. 3. pp. 517–527

Rowold, J. (2008). Effects of Transactional and Transformational Leadership of Pastors. *Pastoral Psychol, 56,* 403–411

Salwen, E., Underwood, L., Dy-Liacco, G., & Arveson, K. (2017). Self-Disclosure and Spiritual Well-Being in Pastors Seeking Professional Psychological Help. *Pastoral Psychol, 66,* 505–521

Sanders, J. (2007). Spiritual Leadership. Principles of Excellency for Every Believer. Chicago, IL: Moody Publishers

Scazzero, P., Bird, W. (2010). The Emotionally Healthy Church. A Strategy for Discipleship That Actually Changes Lives. Updated and Expanded Edition. Grand Rapids, MI: Zondervan

Scharen, C., Campbell-Reed, E. (2017). By Grace and by Grit. How New Pastors Learn in Practice. *In Trust*

Schuhmann, C., Geugten, W. (2017). Believable Visions of the Good: An Exploration of the Role of Pastoral Counselors in PromotingRresilience. *Pastoral Psychol, (66),* 523–536

Scott G. & Lovell, R. (2015). The Rural Pastors Initiative: Addressing Isolation and Burnout in Rural Ministry. *Pastoral Psychol (2015)* 64:71–97 DOI 10.1007/s11089-013-0591-z

Sneglar, R., Renard, M., Stacy (2017). Preventing Compassion Fatigue Amongst Pastors: The Influence of Spiritual Intelligence and Intrinsic Motivation. *Journal of Psychology & Theology, 45,* 4, 247–260

Staley, R., McMinn, M., Gathercoal, K., Free, K. (2012). Strategies Employed By Clergy to Prevent and Cope with Interpersonal Isolation. *Pastoral Psychol, 62,* 843–857

Sparkman, T. (2017). The Leadership Development Experiences of Church Denomination Executives. *The Journal of Applied Christian Leadership, 11* (1)

Spencer, J., Winston, B., & Bocarnea, M. (2012). Predicting the Level of Pastors' Risk of Termination/Exit from the Church. *Pastoral Psychol (2012)* 61:85–98 DOI 10.1007/s11089-011-0410-3

Steiner, S. (2009). Thriving Pastors, Thriving Congregations. *Canadian Mennonite.* Pastoral Trends Survey Report: Part I or IV

Stewart. K. (2009). Keeping Your Pastor: An Emerging Challenge. *Journal for the Liberal Arts and Sciences, 13* (3)

Strunk, J., Milacci, F., Zabloski, J. (2017). The Convergence of Ministry, Tenure, and Efficacy: Beyond Speculation Toward a New Theory of Pastoral Efficacy. *Pastoral Psychol, 66,* 537–550

Sword, W. (1999). Pearls, Pith, Provocation. Accounting for Presence of Self: Reflections On Doing Qualitative Research. Qualitative Health Research, *9 (2)* 270–278

Tan, S. (2019). Shepherding God's People. A Guide to Faithful and Fruitful Pastoral Ministry. Grand Rapids, MI: Baker Publishing Group

Thrall, B., McNicol, B., McElrath, K. (1999). The Ascent of a Leader. How Ordinary Relationships Develop Extraordinary Character and Influence. San Francisco, CA: Jossey-Bass

Tucker, C. (2017). Calvin and the Call To Ministry. *The Reformed Theological Review, (76)* 2

Vaccarino, F. (2013). Exploring Clergy Self-care: A New Zealand Study. *The International Journal of Religion and Spirituality in Society, 3*

Visker, J., Rider, T., Humpbres-Ginther, A. (2017). Ministry-Related Burnout and Stress Coping Mechanisms Among Assemblies of God-ordained Clergy in Minnesota. *J Relog Health 53*: 951–961

Voltmer, F. Thomas, C. & Spahn, C. (2011). Psychological Health and Spirituality of Theology Students and Pastors of the German Seventh-Day Adventist Church. *Review of Religious Research 52, 3:* 290–305

Wells, C., Probst, J., McKeown, R. (2011). The Relationship Between Work-related Stress and Boundary-related Stress Within the Clerical Profession. *J. Jelig Health*, 51: 215–230

Wertz, F. (2005). Phenomenological Research Methods for Counseling Psychology. *Journal of Counseling Psychology, 52*(2), 167–177

West, J. (2016). An Analysis of Emotional Intelligence Training and Pastoral Job Satisfaction. *Journal of Pastoral Care & Counseling, 70* (4), 228–243

Wilson, M., Hoffman, B. (2007). *Preventing Ministry Failure. A Shepherdcare Guide for Pastors, Ministers and other Caregivers.* Downers Grove, IL. InterVarsity Press

www.usachurches.org

Yin, R. (2011). *Qualitative Research From Start to Finish.* New York, NY. The Guilford Press

Young, J., Firmin, M. (2014). Qualitative Perspectives Toward Relational Connection in Pastoral Ministry. 19, #Art 93, 1–14

BIOGRAPHY OF
DR. TERENCE O. HAYES, SR.

Pastor Terence O. Hayes, Sr. was born on October 20th, 1961 in the city of Dayton, OH. An honor graduate from the class of 1979, he attended John H. Patterson High School where he studied Distributive Education in wholesaling and retailing. He is also an inductee in the National Honor Society.

Terence served over 21 years in the United States Air Force and retired in July 2002. He served 20 years at Wright Patterson Air Force Base as an Administrative Specialist and completed a one year tour in the Republic of Korea at Osan Air Base as an Executive officer. Upon his retirement, he was awarded several distinctive medals, including The Meritorious Service Medal and The Air Force Commendation Medal with 5 oak leaf clusters. He was also awarded the Outstanding Volunteer Service Medal for his off-duty involvement in the local community; specifically for his work with the gospel group, New Harvest. As the visionary and creator of the group, Terence devoted over 1000 hours over 18 years of mentoring and being a role model to the young men he worked with.

May 2004, Terence was appointed as Senior Pastor of Faith Deliverance Church of God in Christ. He assumed the role of leadership after the founder, Superintendent Norman McDuffie entered the role as Emeritus Pastor after twenty four years of ministry. His astute administrative skills, contagious personality, and willingness to serve God and his congregation are a testament to his heartfelt leadership skills. Pastor Hayes's favorite passage of scripture is, "where there is no vision, the people would perish: but he that keepeth the law, happy is he" (Proverbs 29:18).

Terence's greatest passion is his love and commitment to gospel music. As a songwriter and arranger, he has numerous songs built into his writing repertoire. Besides, several of his works are associated with the Broadcast Music Incorporation (BMI) music group association. In 2013 the group, New Harvest under his leadership was honored to be named "Dayton's Originals" in the historical archives of the city of Dayton. New Harvest made its debut in 2005 at the famed Showtime at the Apollo in New York City. A history-making experience in itself, the group further excelled in 2008 as 3-time Dove Award Nominees for the self-titled project, "New Harvest." Their self-titled maxi-single, "The Strength of a Man," written and arranged by Terence O. Hayes, Jr., was the first musical work from FaithWorks Records, & "The Best of New Harvest" in digital outlets. In 2013, movie producer Robert Townsend featured their hit single, "I Can't Stop," in his Entertainment One movie, "The Hive."

Terence is a bi-vocational pastor; currently a Supply Technician for Foreign Military Sales at Wright Patterson Air Force Base, OH. He is a graduate of Liberty University with an Educational Doctoral Degree in Community Care and Counseling, with a cognate in Pastoral Counseling, Master of Arts in Pastoral Counseling, Bachelors of Science degree in Psychology, with a concentration in Christian Counseling, Associate Degree in Psychology-Christian Counseling. In 2014 he was selected as one of the Church of God in Christ's 100 Influential Pastors. Terence received the Dr. Martin Luther King Humanitarian Award in February of 2021 from Wright Patterson Air Force Base, OH. He's also a member of the American Association of Christian Counselors and was recently selected to join The Society for Collegiate Leadership & Achievement with a 3.86 GPA. Dr. Hayes established The Ethel Hayes Destigmatization of Mental Health Scholarship.

Terence is married to Rhonda L. McDuffie-Hayes. They were joined in holy matrimony on January 26th, 1980. They are the proud parents of five daughters and two sons, two sons-in-law, two-daughter-in-laws, and a host of grandchildren.

Printed in the United States
by Baker & Taylor Publisher Services